English Reading Treasures

Hyon-Sue Kim

BAEKSAN
Publishing Co.

AUTHOR

- **Hyon-Sue Kim(김현수)**

경희대학교 영어영문학 학사/석사/박사
Brookdale Community College (New Jersey, U.S.A.) 수료
Berlitz Language School (Ohio, U.S.A.) Translator
장안대학 외국어계열 영어통역과 교수 (1983~현재)

〈저서〉
English Reading Adventure
English Reading for College Student
Prospective English Reading(공저)
Situational Conversation(공저)
Essential English(공저)
Tourism English Reading
Practical English for Flight Attendants(공저)

〈논문〉
즈네뜨(G. Genette)의 시간이론으로 본 포크너(Wm. Faulkner)의
〈압살롬, 압살롬!〉(Absalom, Absalom!) 외 다수

English Reading Treasures

Baeksan Publishing Co.
653-40, Jeongreung3-dong, Seongbuk-gu,
Seoul, #136-852, Korea

ISBN 978-89-6183-266-3

Printed in Korea 2010.
※ 저자와 합의로 인지첩부 생략함.
※ 책값 15,000원

I.n.t.r.o.d.u.c.t.i.o.n

대학교육 과정(curriculum) 중에서 '영어 강독'이 최근에 '영어 읽기'나 '영어 읽기와 이해'로 명칭이 변경되었다. 내용이 아무리 좋아도 너무 난해하거나 긴 내용들은 접근을 기피하는 최근의 현상들 때문에 과목의 명칭 변경뿐만 아니라 교재의 '다시 쓰기'가 절실히 필요했다.

대학 교수로 '영어 읽기'를 25년이 넘도록 강의해 온 경험을 바탕으로, 유익하면서도 재미있는 내용과 난이도의 균형의 조화를 배려하여, 학생들이 강의를 들으면서 호기심을 가지고 재미있게 공부할 수 있도록 편집하였다. 또한 시각적 효과로 학습동기를 가능한 한 최대한 유발하기 위하여 각 과(unit)의 주제와 관련된 사진들을 많이 수록하여 편집하였다.

각 과(unit)들을 공부하면서 어휘(vocabulary), 숙어(idiom), 문법(grammar)을 비롯한 학문적 성취는 물론이고, 학생들의 인성도 훌륭하게 빚어져 갈 수 있었으면 하는 바람도 담아 보았다.

각 과들은 본문과 Exercise I~V(과에 따라서는 I~VI, VII)로 구성되어 있고, 이 Exercise들은 각 과를 정리하기 위한 목적으로 강의 시간 또는 평소 테스트용으로도 사용이 가능하다. 각 과들의 본문과 Exercise 문항들을 계속 학습함으로써 토익(TOEIC), 토플(TOEFL)의 Reading Comprehension을 위한 철저한 대비는 물론이고, 영어 전공자로서의 기본적인 실력이 반드시 향상될 것을 기대하며 확신해 마지않는다.

이 책이 출판되기까지 수고해 주신 백산출판사의 진욱상 사장님과 편집부 여러분들, 교재에 쓸 사진들을 여행 때마다 열심히 찍어 주고 컴퓨터의 기술적인 문제들을 늘 도와준 유완영 박사님, 그리고 성실하게 많은 도움을 준 최은아 선생님에게 감사한 마음을 전합니다.

김현수

C.o.n.t.e.n.t.s

English Reading Treasures

1

Our Better Sides

English Reading Treasures 1

Our Better Sides

Fred C. Kelly

When we don't like a man it is usually not because we know him. It's because we don't know him. It is hard to dislike many people after we get to know them better.

I've known policemen and detectives who became friendly with the crooks[1) they had to capture. And I've known a few criminals who weren't angry at the jury or the judge who put them in jail. They knew they had done wrong and that the jury and judge were doing their honest duty.

This may not happen all the time. But most of us know the old story

1) crooks : dishonest person or a criminal. 도둑, 사기꾼.

about cats and dogs. They are not supposed to like each other. Most of the time they don't. But when they grow up in the same house they may get along fine.

We sometimes feel unfriendly toward people from other countries or people who are of a different race or religion. I don't think this bad feeling is really something personal. I think it's because the stranger has customs and ways that are not like our town.

I'll never forget Mr. Davis in my home town. He was the richest man in our town. He had a funny kind of walk. He carried himself[2) with his head and chin up and with his shoulders thrown back like an Army officer. This is all right if you are in the Army, but he wasn't in the Army. He was a business man, and we thought he was stuck-up. Nearly everybody in town hated him.

I was a reporter on the town paper and saw Mr. Davis nearly every day. He never spoke when he passed us on the street. He just marched along, eyes front, chin up and stomach in. I wrote a couple of funny stories about him, poked fun at him whenever I had the chance.

Our bank failed during the depression.[3) Mr. Davis was put in charge of it. I was supposed to get the story about the bank failure

2) carry oneself : walk and move in that way. 행동하다, ~의 자세를 취하다.

3) the depression : a time when there is very little economic activity, which causes a lot of unemployment and poverty. 1929년 미국의 경제 공황기.

from him. It took me a long time to get the nerve to call on him.[4)] After all the mean things that I had printed about him I expected him to slam the door in my face.[5)] But I had to get the story so I took a chance.[6)] I called at the bank.

I was surprised. He didn't slam the door in my face. He was very nice to me.

"It's a long story," he told me, when I asked about the bank. "We'd better go up to the library where we can talk." I went with him to his library where he gave me the whole story.

He told me how the bank was robbed by the people who worked in it. A lot of his story was too hard for me to understand because I did not know how a bank was operated. I knew about the newspaper business but not about banks. He took extra time to explain the things that puzzled me and no matter how dumb I seemed, he tried to help me understand. When he finished I really understood why the bank had failed. I also felt sorry about the stories I had printed.

"I envy you newspaper men," said Mr. Davis. "You have a chance to get around and really know everybody. I've always wanted to

4) It took... nerve to call on him : 그를 찾아갈 용기를 얻는데 꽤나 시간이 걸렸다, 몹시 망설였다.

5) slam the door in one's face : 문전박대를 하다.

6) take a (one's) chance : 헛수고인 줄 알면서도 한번 시도해 보다.

know people, too. But I'm nearsighted[7] and can't see far enough to know people when I meet them on the street. I feel shy about meeting people for that reason. It's something I've never been able to get over. So you see, I know very few people in town."

Really Mr. Davis was a very nice fellow. He wanted to have friends. He had learned to walk like an Army officer and we just thought he was stuck-up. After we learned what kind of a man he really was, we liked him.

– From *The Fun of Knowing Folks* by Fred C. Kelly

7) nearsighted : cannot see distant things clearly. 근시안적인, 소견이 좁은.

Exercises

I. Read the following paragraph and answer the questions.

I'll never forget Mr. Davis in my home town. He was the richest man in our town. He had a funny kind of walk. (1)He carried himself with his head and chin up and with his shoulders thrown back like an Army officer. This is all right if you are in the Army, but he wasn't in the Army. He was a business man, and we thought he was stuck-up. Nearly everybody in town hated him.

1. What was the name of the richest man in town?
2. Was he an Army officer?
3. What kind of walk did he have?
4. How did they think of him?
5. Translate (1) into Korean.

II. Fill each blank with one of the words given below.

at	on	along	in	over

6. When they grow up in the same house they may get (   ) fine.
7. There are a few criminals who weren't angry (   ) the judge.
8. It took me along time to get a nerve to call (   ) him.
9. It's something I've never been able to get (   ).
10. This is all right if you are (   ) the Army.

III. Match the words with the corresponding definitions.

11. depression	a. a time when there is very little economic activity
12. slam	b. can not see distant things clearly
13. crook	c. the person in a court of law
14. nearsighted	d. shut noisily and with great force.
15. judge	e. a dishonest person or a criminal

IV. Read the statements below and write T if it is true ; write F if it is false.

16. Mr. Davis was a reporter on the town paper. (   )
17. When we don't like somebody, it's because we don't know him. (   )
18. Nearly everybody in town liked Mr. Davis. (   )
19. Mr. Davis was in charge of the bank failure. (   )
20. Mr. Davis was nearsighted and can't see far enough. (   )

V. Choose the word or phrase that best completes each sentence. Change the form of the verbs if necessary.

poke	chance	crooks	make	charge

21. I've known some policemen who became friendly with the __________ they had to capture.
22. I wrote some funny stories about him __________ fun at him.
23. Mr. Davis was in __________ of the bank failure.
24. I had to get the story so I took a __________.
25. I've learned that we all can __________ mistakes with people.

English Reading Treasures

2

On Achieving Success ; On Love and Women

English Reading Treasures 2

On Achieving Success ; On Love and Women

E. Hemingway[1)]

On Achieving Success

We cannot travel every path. Success must be won along one line. We must make our business the one life purpose to which every other must be subordinate[2)].

I hate a thing done by halves. If it be right, do it boldly : if it be wrong, leave it undone.

To live with ideal is a successful life. It is not what one does, but what one tries to do, that makes a man strong.

"Eternal vigilance,"[3)] it has been said, "is the price of liberty." With equal truth it may be said, "unceasing effort is the price of

1) Ernest Hemingway (1898~1961) : 미국의 소설가. 1954년 노벨문학상 수상.

2) subordinate : to place in a lower rank or class. 하급의, 부차적인.

3) vigilance : very careful to notice any signs of danger or trouble. 경계, 조심.

success." If we do not work with our might,[4] others will : and they will outstrip us in the race, and pluck[5] the prize from our grasp.

Success grows less and less dependent on luck and chance. Self-distrust is the cause of most of our failures.

The great and indispensable help to success is character. Character is crystallized habit, the result of training and conviction. Every character is influenced by the heredity, environment and education. But these apart, if every man were not to a great extent the architect of his own character, he would be a fatalist,[6] an irresponsible creature of circumstances.

On Love and Women

Love is the greatest adventure in people's lives. The heart is the noblest part of human nature. And the affections are the noblest ingredients in human nature.

Once while hearing a young lady highly praised for her beauty, I asked : What kind of beauty do you mean? Merely that of the

4) with all one's might : 전력을 다하다.

5) pluck : take it between your fingers and pull it in order to remove it from its stalk where it is growing. 잡아뜯다, 잡아당기다, 움켜쥐다.

6) fatalist : determinist. 운명론자.

body, or also that of the mind? Many a pretty girl is like a flower which is admired for[7] its beautiful appearance, but despised for its unpleasant odor. It is far better to acquire beauty than to be born with it.

No wise person will marry for beauty mainly. It may exercise a powerful attraction in the first place, but it is found to be of comparatively little consequence afterwards. To marry a handsome figure without character, fine features unbeautified by sentiment or good nature, is the most deplorable[8] of mistakes. As even the finest landscape, seen daily, becomes monotonous, so does the most beautiful face, unless a beautiful nature shines through it. The beauty of today becomes commonplace tomorrow. Whereas goodness, displayed through the most ordinary features, is perennially[9] lovely. This kind of beauty improves with age, and time ripens rather than destroys it.

---

7) be admired for : ~ 때문에 칭찬받다, 칭송받다.

8) deplorable : lamentable. 한탄할 만한, 개탄할 만한.

9) perennially : perpetually. 영원히.

A man should never be too precisely analytical of a woman. Silence is often the best ornament of a woman.

On Living with Honor

It is desirable to have a good reputation. The good opinion of our associates and acquaintances is not to be despised. There is often a great distinction between character and reputation. Reputation is what the world believes us for the time ; character is what we truly are. Reputation and character may be in harmony, but they frequently are as opposite as light and darkness.

The best equipment a young man can have for the battle of life is a conscience, common sense and good health. There is no friend so good as a good conscience. There is no enemy so dangerous as a bad conscience. It makes us either kings or slaves.

Anger is a short madness. There is in it envy and scorn, fear and sorrow, pride and prejudice, rashness and inconsideration.

Ambition destroys the pleasures of the present in ardent aspirations after an imaginative future. Contempt is an innocent revenge. Violence is the fullest expression of it.

Anxiety is the poison of human life. It is the parent of many miseries.

– From *Advice to a Young Man* by Hemingway

Exercises

I. Read the following paragraph and answer the questions.

"Eternal vigilance," it has been said, "is the price of liberty." With equal truth it may be said, (1)"unceasing effort is the price of success." If we do not work (2)with our might, others will : and they will outstrip us in the race, and pluck the prize from our grasp. Success grows less and less dependent on luck and chance. Self-distrust is the cause of most of our failures.

1. What is the meaning of "vigilance"?
2. What is the cause of most of our failure?
3. What does (1) mean?
4. What is the price of success?
5. Translate (2) into Korean.

II. Fill each blank with one of the words given below.

in	or	for	by	as	with

6. Many a pretty girl is admired ( ) its beautiful appearance.
7. Reputation and character may be ( ) harmony.
8. It makes us either kings ( ) slaves.
9. They frequently are as opposite ( ) light and darkness.
10. I hate a thing done ( ) halves.
11. This kind of beauty improves ( ) age.
12. No wise person will marry ( ) beauty mainly.

III. Match the words with the corresponding definitions.

13. fatalist	a. lamentable
14. vigilance	b. determinist
15. perennially	c. very careful to notice any signs of danger
16. subordinate	d. perpetually
17. deplorable	e. to place in a lower rank or class

IV. Read the following statements and write T if it is true, write F if it is false.

18. We can travel every path. (   )
19. Beauty may exercise a powerful attraction all the time. (   )
20. Success must be won along one line. (   )
21. A man should be very precisely analytical of a woman. (   )
22. The beauty of today becomes commonplace tomorrow. (   )
23. There are many friends so good as a good conscience. (   )
24. To live with ideal is dangerous for a successful life. (   )
25. Silence is often the best ornament of a woman. (   )

V. Choose the word or phrase that best completes each sentence. Change the form of the verbs if necessary.

for	be	dependent	ornament	between

26. If it __________ right, do it boldly.
27. Reputation is what the word believes us __________ the time.
28. There is often a great distinction __________ character and reputation.
29. Success grows less and less __________ on luck and chance.
30. Silence is often the best __________ of a woman.

English Reading Treasures

3

How to Enjoy Music

English Reading Treasures 3

How to Enjoy Music

George R. Marek[1]

That morning, I was sure the end of the world had come. My boss had fired[2] me ; and with the pessimism of youth, I was convinced that I would never find another job. I was marked for[3] failure. (I was 19 years old.)

That evening I had a date to meet a friend at Lewisohn Stadium, to hear the New York Philharmonic. Job or no job, I decided to go.

At first, as I sat there, the music merely lapped against the stone wall of my anxiety. But with the final number of the program, the

1) George R. Marek (1902~1987) : Vienna 태생의 미국 음악평론가.

2) fire : v. to force somebody to leave their job ; discharge ; dismiss. 해고시키다.

3) be marked for : be destined to+명사. ~할 운명이다.

"First Symphony" of Brahms, I began to listen in earnest[4]. As the music reached me, I reflected that I had heard the symphony often before, that I was probably to hear it often again under different conditions and that it always had been, and would be in the future, the same satisfying music. It did not change ; only I did. I was impermanent ; the symphony was permanent. I drew comfort from this.

I measured the event of the day more calmly. Was it as important as all that? Couldn't I do something about it? As I walked home, the dull blanket of despondency[5] weighed less. Somehow I would manage to find another job.

Since then, I have often marveled at[6] the power that lies in music to raise the spirits, to comfort shaken nerves, to serve as a rope can lift itself. I am, of course, not the first to marvel. Most of us remember Congreve's "Music hath charms to soothe[7] the savage beast." Horace spoke of music as "the healing balm of troubles." I feel physically refreshed and strengthened by it," said Coleridge. Even Goethe, who was not particularly musical, said that music made him unfold like the fingers of a threatening fist which straighten, amicably.

---

4) in earnest : adj. very serious and sincere. 진지한, 열심인.

5) despondency : n. low spirits ; dejection. 낙담, 의기소침.

6) marvel at : v. ~ at sth to be very surprised or impressed by sth. ~에 놀라다, 경탄하다.

7) soothe : v. to bring relief from (a pain, etc.) ; to allay, comfort. 달래다, 진정시키다.

Music may be used in two different ways. The first way is the road taken by music lover. He need not be able to tell a fugue from a fandango[8]. But to him, the hearing of music is an experience that grips his mind and tears at his heart. He cannot remain indifferent.

How does one become a music lover? There is but one way : Listen to music! Only direct experience, not study or explanations or any sort of prop[9], will lead you to music.

I have two suggestions for the beginner. First, listen to the same composition often, until you can respond to it emotionally. Do

---

8) tell a fugue from fandango : v. tell~from~ to distinguish one thing or person from another. 분간하다, 구별[식별]하다 ; fugue=둔주곡 ; fandango=활기찬 스페니시 아메리칸 뮤직.

9) prop : n. (劇) property, illustrative device. 소도구, 의상.

not expect to encompass a symphony at first hearing. And do not be discouraged or feel guilty if, while listening to an unfamiliar symphony, your attention wanders. Initially, absorb from it as much as you can - and coast through the rest. There will be a time when the clouds roll away and the landscape lies clearly before you. In music, the familiar is the enjoyable. Don't dart[10] from one composition to the next. Stay with it!

Second, choose - in the beginning at least, - romantic music. This is repertoire that begins with Beethoven and ends with Sibelius and that, in its wide orbit, includes the most popular works - those of Schubert, Brahms, Dvorak, Tchaikovsky, Verdi, Wagner, Berlioz and

10) dart : v. to move suddenly and fast ; spring, dash. 돌진하다.

a dozen other composers[11)] of the 19th century. Such music, with its rich coloring, its exuberance, its sweetness, its exciting oratory, makes an immediate appeal[12)].

But it is not safe to predict what you will like. We do know that people tend to respond more easily to Chopin and Puccini than to Handel or Haydn. Yet your experience may differ.

Of all the arts, music is the freest. Most music does not "mean" anything except in its own world and on its own terms. But because it has little to do with what we call real life, because it is free of the weekday, it can effectively take us away from our own lives, from our nine-to-five worries[13)]. Because music travels on winged feet, it can make us forget where the shoe pinches[14)].

– From *How to Enjoy Music* by George R. Marek

11) composer : n. a person who writes music, especially classical music. 작곡가.
12) make an appeal : to be attractive, interesting, pleasing etc. 호소하다, 매혹하다.
13) nine-to-five worries : problems of a regular job. 오전 9시부터 오후 5시까지의 걱정거리.
14) pinch : v. hurt because it is too tight. (구두 등이) 죄어 아프다.

Exercises

I. Read the following paragraph and answer the questions.

That morning, I was sure the end of the world had come. My boss had fired me ; and with the pessimism of youth, I was convinced that I would never find another job. I was marked for failure. (I was 19 years old.) That evening I had a date to meet a friend at Lewisohn Stadium, to hear the New York Philharmonic. Job or no job, I decided to go. At first, as I sat there, (1)the music merely lapped against the stone wall of my anxiety. But with the final number of the program, the "First Symphony" of Brahms, I began to listen (2)in earnest.

1. Why did the author feel that the world has come to the end?
2. At what age did the author get laid off from his job?
3. Where did he meet his friend to hear the New York Philharmonic?
4. What does (1) mean? Explain.
5. Translate (2) into Korean.

II. Fill each blank with one of the words given below.

to	at	for	with	from	in

6. I was marked ( ) failure.
7. But with the final number of the program, I began to listen ( ) earnest.
8. Since then, I have often marveled ( ) the power that lies in music.
9. He need not be able to tell a fugue ( ) a fandango.
10. First, listen ( ) the same composition often, until you can respond to it emotionally.
11. Don't dart from one composition to the next. Stay ( ) it!

III. Match the word or expression with its definition.

12. dart	a. to force somebody to leave their job
13. composition	b. make sure, believe firmly
14. encompass	c. a specific written or musical work. a piece of music
15. fire	d. to move suddenly and fast ; spring ; dash
16. convince	e. to surround or cover something completely

IV. Choose the closest meaning to the following words.

17. despondency

a. respond　　b. dejection

c. irritation　　d. repression

18. earnest

a. sincere　　b. carless

c. kind　　d. honest

19. soothe

a. smooth　　b. comfort

c. watch　　d. sue

20. composition

a. paragraph　　b. a musical piece

c. construction　　d. building

21. dart(v)

a. dash　　b. narrow

c. head　　d. dance

V. Choose the word or phrase that best completes each sentence.

Coleridge	Goethe	romantic	appeal	tears at

22. The author suggests to the beginner of music to choose __________ music.
23. __________ felt physically refreshed and strengthened by music.
24. __________ said that music made him unfold like the fingers of a threatening fist which straighten, amicably.
25. To the music lover music is an experience that grips his mind and __________ his heart.
26. Romantic music, with its rich coloring, its exuberance, its sweetness, its exciting oratory, makes an immediate __________.

VI. Choose the correct answer for each question.

27. According to the author the music can help us __________

    a. to tense. b. to get a job.

    c. to heal our physical wounds. d. to soothe our feelings.

28. The author decided __________even though he got fired from his job.

a. not to meet his friends
b. to go to the orchestra
c. to visit his boss
d. no to go the orchestra

29. Who has mentioned that music is the healing balm of troubles?

a. Congreve
b. Horace
c. Coleridge
d. Goethe

30. The author suggests to the beginner of music to______

a. listen to the same composition often.
b. study any sort of prop.
c. try to encompass a symphony.
d. listen to all kinds of music once.

VII. Mark each sentence as either true(T) or false(F) according to the text.

31. "The music merely lapped against the stone wall of my anxiety" means the author didn't listen to music in earnest at first. (   )
32. Listening to the First Symphony by Brahms helped the author to overcome the despondency he was feeling after getting laid off. (   )
33. The author was the only one who was marveled at the power of music. (   )
34. To become a music lover one has to study music. (   )
35. The beginner of music should choose romantic music at first. (   )

English Reading Treasures

4

Word Wizards

English Reading Treasures
4

Word Wizards[1)]

It's bee season! Sensational spellers win their way to the 2004 final

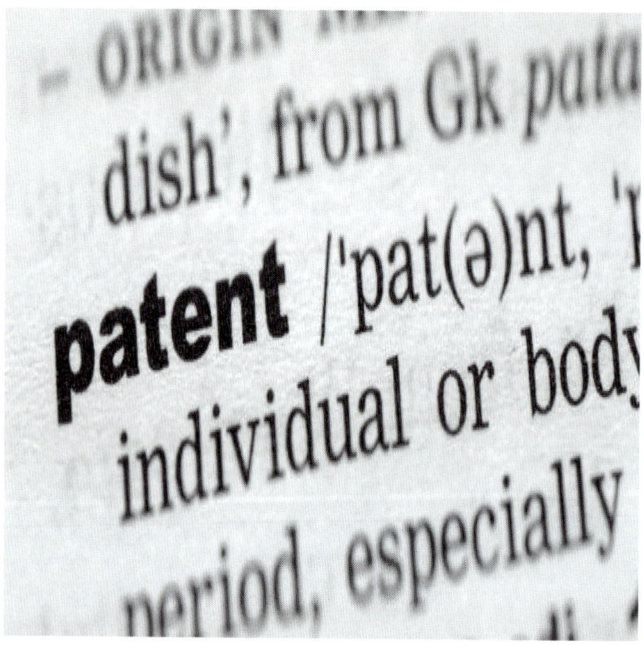

The moment had arrived. After hundreds of hours spent studying thousands of words, only six letters stood between Erik Zyman Carrasco, 12 and a third trip to the Scripps National Spelling Bee[2)].

---

1) wizard : n. a man who has magic powers. 마법사.

2) bee : n. a social event where people get together for a competition or to do something such as sew. 모임.

would all that time poring over his dictionary pay off[3] again this year? After a deep breath, Erik spelled "z-e-p-h-y-r," then pump[4]ed his fists in jubilation[5]. Erik's win, in New york City on March 23, 2004, enables him to join 263 other regional champs, who will all compete at the 77th-annual nations in Washington, D.C.

"There won't be much pressure, because being there means you're already a champion," Erik said. Even so, his goal is to win the $12,000 first prize. He placed seventh last year and 10th two years ago. Erik is one of more than 10 million kids nationwide who take part in spelling bees every year. At the national bee, super spellers in eighth grade or lower represent Jamaica, Mexico, Puerto Rico, the Bahamas and every state except Vermont. One recent competitor was only 8 years old! The finalists compete in front of 1,000 people and an ESPN[6] television audience of millions.

Tough Competition

One of the spellers going up against Erik will be Brady Yoon, 14,

3) pay off : to be successful and bring good results. 이익을 가져오다, 성과를 거두다.
4) pump : v. to move sth quickly up and down or in and out. 올리다.
5) jubilation : n. a feeling of great happiness and pleasure, because of a success. 환희, 환호.
6) ESPN : a US cable television sports network. 미국 케이블 방송.

of Anaheim Hills, California. Brady beat out some 500 kids from his school and about 50 winners from other California schools to qualify for the all-expense-paid trip to Washington, D.C. Brady's older sister made it to the national bee in 1998. More than 25 of the spellers who qualified for this year's bee have siblings[7)] who have competed at the nationals.

In addition to spelling, Brady participates in the Science Olympiad and in academic pentathlons[8)]. Like many outstanding spellers, Brady excels at multiple activities. Spelling champs study

7) sibling : n. a brothers and sisters. 형제, 자매.

8) pentathlon : n. an athletics competition in which each person must compete in five different events. 5종 경기.

an overage of five to 15 hours a week. Some of that time is spent mastering lists of difficult words. But most spellers also practice word sleuthing[9]. That means they learn to use language clues to figure out[10] the spelling of unfamiliar words.

Spelling Traditions

Spelling bees date to the 1700s. They have almost always been in English, says Paige Kimble, the director of the National Spelling Bee- and the 1981 champion. "In almost all other languages, words are spelled how they sound," she says. For most kids who participate[11] in bees at local level, going to the nationals isn't everything. Many kids just enjoy the chance to learn new words and to gain confidence in front an audience.

Eleven-year-old Jonathan Cohen of Rhode Island won his school bee as a fourth grader last year. But he didn't do well enough in the state's bee to qualify[12] for this year's nationals. He plans to try again next year, when he's in the sixth grade. "I really like the complexity

9) sleuthing : n. the investigation of a crime or mystery by someone who is not a police officer. 추적, 조사.

10) figure out : to think about sb/sth until you understand them. 이해하다, 해결하다.

11) participate : v. to take part in or become involved in an activity. 참여하다, 관여하다.

12) qualify : to be of a high enough standard to enter a competition. 자격을 주다.

of the English language," Jonathan says, "and how there are so many different ways to spell a word. That challenge is what makes it fun."

Think!

How would you prepare for a spelling contest? Which of the words that you use are the hardest to spell? Many bees pick words from a book called Paideia. Spellers study it to prepare. The book lists more than 3,600 words. The five below are not the toughest, but they're the ones most often tested at competitions. Quiz your friends to see how well they can spell.

The Latest Lingo - How new words make it into the dictionary

Do you Google in the snain? Don't bother[13] to look for these words in Merriam-Webster's Collegiate Dictionary. Snain, meaning "a mix of snow and rain," never caught on, Google, meaning "to search the Internet," may be added in 2006. Some 1,000 new words or usages enter the English language each year. Some go

13) bother : v. (negative) to spend time and/or energy doing sth. 방해하다.

into the dictionary. Others fade from use. "Our language is a living thing," Jim Lowe, an editor at Merriam-Webmaster, says. "It keeps growing."

Merriam-Webster first published the Collegiate Dictionary in 1898. Since then, at least 100,000 words have been added. As the world changes, we need new words to describe it. The dictionary's editors look in everything from catalogs to comic books for the latest lingo. New words go on index cards[14] that note when and where they first appeared.

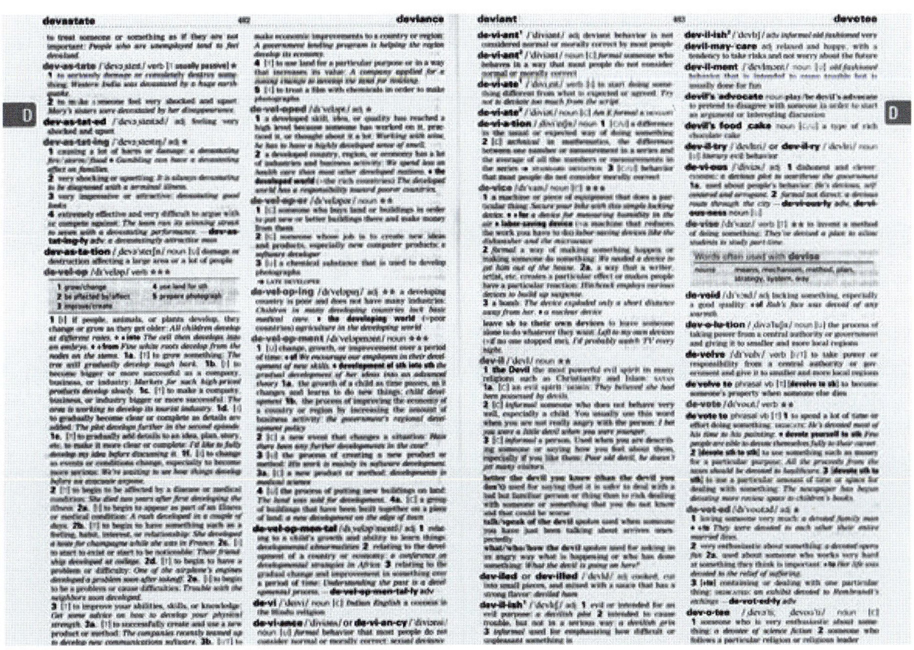

14) index card : n. a small card that you can write information on and keep with other cards in a box or file. 색인 카드.

Lowe reviews these words for the edition's annual updates. Every 10 years, the dictionary gets a total makeover[15]. Lowe and the other editors review the one million or so new terms they have found. About 10,000 make it in. For a word to be added, it must show up regularly in a lot of places. Lowe is no

longer surprised by the words he finds. "When I first saw spam[16], I thought it was unusual," he says. "It's hard to associate meats with e-mail." but there it is on page 1,195, in black and white.

– From *Topics for In-depth Reading*, Time - H&B Press, 2007

15) makeover : n. the process of improving the appearance of a person or a place. 변모, 개선.

16) spam : n. In computing, to spam people or organizations means to send unwanted e-mails to a large number of them, usually as advertising. 스팸 메일.

Exercises

I. Read the following paragraph and answer the questions.

The moment had arrived. (1)After hundreds of hours spent studying thousands of words, only six letters stood between ErikZyman-Carrasco, 12, and a third trip to the Scripps National Spelling Bee. Would all that time poring over his dictionary pay off again this year? After a deep breath, Erik spelled (2)"z-e-p-h-y-r," then pumped his fists in (3)jubilation.

1. What is the name of the contest Erik participated in?
2. How old is Erik?
3. What is the meaning of "zephyr"?
4. What is the synonym of (3) jubilation?
5. Translate (1) into Korean.

II. Match the words with the corresponding definitions.

6. lingo	a. the upbringing of a child
7. paideia	b. a person who is good at something
8. sleuthing	c. a brother or sister
9. sibling	d. a jargon
10. wizard	e. an act of investigating an event

III. Read the following statements and write T if it is true ; write F if it is False.

11. Erik is the only one in 10 million kids nationwide who participates in spelling bee every year. (   )
12. Including Brady, spelling champs study 5 to15 hours a week apart from their multifold activities. (   )
13. For may kids who participate in bees at the local level, going to the nationals is everything. (   )
14. About 10,000 new terms are to be added in the dictionary every 10 years. (   )
15. Our language is dead. (   )

IV. Fill each blank with one of the prepositions given below.

off	out	to	in	on	over

16. Erik's win enables him (   ) join 263 other regional champs.
17. Eventually, I shall pay (   ) all my credit card debt.
18. They learn to use language clues to figure (   ) the spelling of the unfamiliar words.
19. New words go (   ) index cards.
20. 'spam' was unusually added on page 1,195 (   ) back and white.

V. Choose the word or phrase that best completes each sentence. Change the form of the verbs if necessary.

Olympiad	qualify	pay off	google	bother	prepare
makeover	lingo	catch on	spam	certify	penthathlong

21. Don't __________ to look for a word like "snain" in the dictionary.
22. It was a total __________ when Mary wore her evening dress for the first time for the annual company party.
23. He didn't do well enough in the state's bee to __________ for the nationals.

24. How would you __________ for the spelling contest?

25. Brady participates in the Science __________.

26. The internet __________ is really interesting.

27. All his hard work __________ during 6month research in the field.

28. Do you __________ when you come across unfamiliar words?

29. It is not always amusing when you find 100 __________ when you check your e-mail.

30. Brady participates in academic __________.

English Reading Treasures

5

Do as the Romans Do

English Reading Treasures
5

Do as the Romans Do

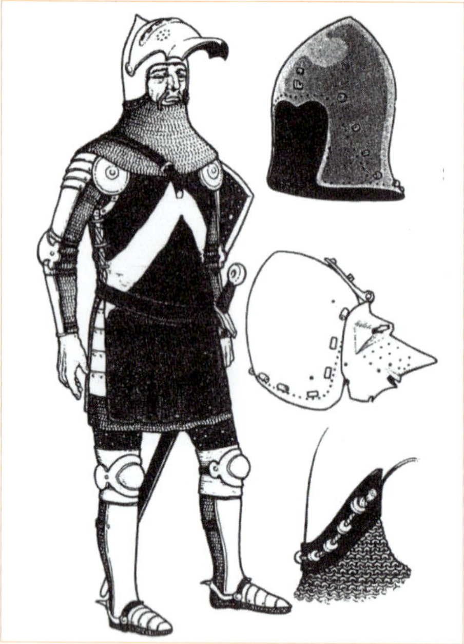

1) Sometimes the rules of etiquette seem to be bothersome, but they are designed to make social relations pleasant. Etiquette is merely acting like a well-bred human being should act. However, the meaning behind some polite customs is not always apparent at first glance. The custom of saluting, for example, stems from the

days when knights wore armor. Their helmets covered their faces to such an extent that it was impossible to recognize even one's best friend. Therefore it became customary[1)] for knights to identify themselves[2)] by lifting the visors of their helmets. Nowadays, the average soldier does not wear a visor, but he still preserves[3)] this old medieval custom by saluting.

2) Shaking hands is another polite custom with an old history. During the Middle Ages it was very dangerous to travel because of robbers that lurked along the roads. Therefore, when two travelers met, they commonly extended their hands to show that they carried no weapons. Today the handshake is merely a sign of our good will and sincerity, but we also express our friendliness by various greetings. Such expressions as "How are you?" and "I hope you're felling well" are designed to express our interest in the welfare of others. Even the word goodbye is a shortened form of "God be with ye." Such expressions stem from man's desire to be friendly and polite.

---

1) customary : used to describe things that people usually do in a particular society or in particular circumstances. 습관적인, 관례의, 통례의.

2) identify oneself : name them or say who or what they are. ~의 정체를 밝히다.

3) preserve : make sure that it remains as it is, and does not change or end. 보호하다, 보존하다, 유지하다.

3) The old saying "When in Rome do as the Romans do" is never more true than when at the dinner table. In some parts of Korea, it is a sign of appreciation to drink one's tea or soup with much gusto[4] and smacking[5] of lips. But in most Western countries no noise should be made while eating.

Eating utensils[6], too, differ from[7] country to country and it is, certainly wise to make a little preliminary study of eating habits before traveling to a foreign country. This precaution can save the traveler a lot of embarrassment.

4) Ignorance of social usage can result in[8] many blunders.[9] A

4) gusto : do it with energetic and enthusiastic enjoyment. 즐김, 기호, 맛, 풍미.
5) smacking : you open and close your mouth noisily, especially before or after eating, to show that you are eager to eat or enjoyed eating. 입맛 다심, 혀차기.
6) utensil : tools or objects that you use in order to help you to cook or to do other tasks in your home. 기구, 용구.
7) differ (from) : unlike each other in some way. 다르다, 의견을 달리하다.
8) result in : a particular situation or event, it causes that situation or event to happen. ~의 결과를 초래하다.
9) blunder : stupid or careless mistake. 큰 실수.

young couple of newlyweds from the country went to New York on their honeymoon. To celebrate the occasion, they decided to have dinner at a fashionable restaurant. The dinner proceeded without incident until almost the end when the waiter placed two small silver bowls of warm water before the bride and groom. To the girl's horror, her husband picked up the dish and to drink the water. Her face turned scarlet as she fervently[10)] hoped that no one had noticed that her husband drank the water in his finger bowl. Later this incident a family joke, but at the time it was no laughing matter.

10) fervently : person has or shows strong feelings about something, and is very sincere and enthusiastic about it. 열렬하게, 강렬하게.

Exercises

I. Read the following paragraph and answer the questions.

The rules of etiquette are designed to make social relations pleasant. (1)Etiquette is acting like a well-bred human being should act. The custom of saluting stems from the days when knights wore armor. They need to identify themselves by lifting the visors of their helmets. Nowadays, this medieval custom becomes (2) ______ . Shaking hands is to show that they carried no weapons in the Middle Ages. Today it means a sign of good will and greetings are come together to be friendly and polite. (3)Smacking of lips at the table is impolite in Western countries.

1. What is the purpose of etiquette?
2. What is etiquette? Translate (1) into Korean.
3. What is the proper word for (2)?
4. What is the purpose of shaking hands?
5. What does (3)Smacking of lips mean? Is it polite in Korea?

II. Fill each blank with one of the prepositions given below.

as	with	for	in	from

6. Therefore it became customary ( ) knights to identify themselves by lifting the visors.
7. Such expressions stem ( ) man's desire to be friendly and polite.
8. When in Rome do ( ) the Romans do.
9. The word goodbye is a shortened form of "God be ( ) ye."
10. Ignorance of social usage can result ( ) many blunders.

III. Match each word with the best meaning.

11. utensil	a. stupid and careless mistake
12. bothersome	b. annoying or irritating
13. smack	c. very polite and good manners
14. well-bred	d. tool especially to cook
15. gusto	e. movable eye part of a helmet
16. blunder	f. wait secretly with bad intention
17. visor	g. enjoyment as in eating or drinking
18. lurk	h. swallow something with a loud noise

IV. Read the following statements and write T if it is true, write F if it is false.

19. The custom of saluting is only for knights. (   )
20. "I hope you're feeling well" means "God be with you." (   )
21. "When in Rome do as the Romans do" is an old saying. (   )
22. All travelers must have some precautions of Rome. (   )
23. A young couple of newly weds went to a restaurant in NY. And the bride drank the water in the finger bowl. (   )
24. The bride's face turned red at the restaurant because of her husband's behavior. (   )

V. Circle the letter of the word that best completes the sentence.

25. The __________ of saluting stems from the old medieval days when knights wore armor.

    a. custom　　b. customary

    c. customer　　d. customs

26. Today the __________ is merely a sign of your goodwill or sincerity.

    a. friend　　b. greetings

    c. handshake　　d. smacking

27. Before traveling to another country, a little __________ study of eating habits is certainly wise.

a. precaution b. preliminary

c. appreciation d. proceed

28. In New York, small silver bowls of warm water is for __________.

a. drinking b. wasting

c. hand washing d. joking

29. In most Western countries noises should not be made while __________.

a. eat b. ate

c. to eat d. eating

30. Etiquette is merely acting like a __________ human being should act.

a. well-being b. wise

c. smart d. well-bred

English Reading Treasures

6

Coffee

English Reading Treasures 6

Coffee

Coffee is one of the most popular beverages[1)] in the world. People drink coffee in Africa, Asia, North and South America, and the Middle East. Coffee has been a part of people's cultures for thousands of years, and today it is still a favorite[2)] drink of millions of people. Do you know the story of coffee and how it became to be so common?

There is an old story that says coffee was discovered in Ethiopia a long, long time ago. A man was watching his goats when he saw them eat some small berries from a tree. After they ate the berries[3)], the goats were lively and active. That night the goats stayed awake

1) beverage : any sort of drink. 마실 것, 음료.

2) favorite : (person or thing) liked best ; regarded with special favor. 마음에 드는, 매우 좋아하는.

3) berry : small seedy fruit, coffee bean. 베리(딸기류의 열매), 장과, 말린 씨앗.

late. Because he often felt tired, the man decided to try the berries. He found that he liked the effect, too.

Coffee spread from Africa to Arabia where it was first used as a medicine and a food before it became a beverage. The Arabs kept coffee a secret for many years. Later, coffee spread to Turkey, then Italy, then France. From Europe, the coffee plant was taken to the new world of America. People discovered that the coffee plant grew well in many parts of South America. Large coffee farms, called plantations[4], were started, and coffee was grown and sent all over the world.

The coffee plant is actually a large shrub, or bush, not really a tree. It can grow very tall (from three to nine meters) if it is left alone in the wild[5]. It has dark green leaves on

4) plantation : a large farm on which cotton, tobacco, sugar, etc. is grown. 농원, 재배지.

5) wild : land in a natural, uncultivated state. 황무지, 야생.

the outside and lighter green leaves underneath. Small white blossoms appear on the leaves, making the coffee plant look like it's covered with snow. After a few days, the fragrant[6)] blossoms[7)] fall off the plant, and small berries begin to grow. The berries change from green to dark red in about six months. Underneath the berry skin there is a green bean. When the berries are ripe, they are picked, and the bean inside is removed. This is the bean that produces coffee.

Coffee beans are picked by hand, one by one. Then they are dried and prepared for market. Coffee beans are shipped[8)] all over the world. When they reach their destination[9)], different coffee beans are blended[10)] together to produce different kinds of coffee. Then the beans are roasted, ground[11)] and packaged[12)] in air-tight cans and bags to keep the coffee fresh. Different countries prefer[13)] different blends. In Turkey and Arabia dark coffee is preferred. In the United States and Canada the coffee is not so dark. Coffee is also prepared and served differently all over the world. In some places it is made

6) fragrant : a. sweet-smelling. 향기로운.

7) blossom : a flower, esp. on a fruit tree. 꽃.

8) ship : to send/put/take in a ship. 배에 싣다, 배로 보내다.

9) destination : a place to which somebody is going (or something is being sent). 목적지, 행선지.

10) blend : to mix together (to get a certain quality). 섞다, 혼합하다.

11) grind - ground - ground : 타다, 갈다, 찧다.

12) package : to put things in a box, bundle, bag, etc. 포장하다, 꾸리다.

13) prefer : to like better. 오히려 ~을 좋아하다.

very thick and strong and served in small cups. Other countries serve coffee with more water in it, in begger cups.

Coffee has become very popular in the United States. Recently, coffee houses and coffee shops have appeared on almost every corner in big cities. These small shops are filled with the smell of fresh-roasted coffee. The tables are full of students, shoppers, and professionals, drinking their favorite kind of coffee. Coffee is now available[14) in flavors[15) such as vanilla and cinnamon, or made with

14) available : capable of being used. 이용할 수 있는.

15) flavor : sensation of taste and smell. 풍미, 향.

hot milk and chocolate. Foreign coffees are also popular. You can order an espresso[16], a cappuccino[17], or a French roast. You can also order "iced coffee" in the summer. Coffee houses are not restaurant, but they usually offer something to eat, often sweets like cookies and cakes. In the United States and all over the world, alone or with family and friends, a cup of coffee gives everyone a moment of enjoyment.

16) espresso : coffee의 일종. 까맣게 볶은 커피 원두에 고압의 증기를 쏘이거나 뜨거운 물을 부어 만드는 쓴맛이 강한 커피.

17) cappuccino : coffee의 일종. espresso coffee에 뜨거운 우유를 탄 것. 종종 cinnamon을 넣고 거품이 있는 크림을 얹어 먹는다.

Exercises

I. Read the following paragraph and answer the questions.

There is an old story that says coffee was discovered in Ethiopia a long, long time ago. Coffee spread from Africa to Arabia where it was first used as a medicine and a food before it became a beverage. (1)The Arabs kept coffee a secret for many years. Later, coffee spread to Turkey, then Italy, then France. From Europe, the coffee plant was taken to the new world of America. People discovered that the coffee plant grew well in many parts of South America. Large coffee farms, called plantations, were started, and coffee was grown and sent all over the world.

1. Where was coffee discovered a long time ago?
2. What was coffee used as first before it became a beverage?
3. From where to where did coffee spread?
4. Translate (1) into Korean.
5. What is plantation?
6. Where did coffee plant grow well?

II. Match the words with the corresponding definitions.

7. beverage	a. sweet and pleasant smell
8. berry	b. to send/put/take in a ship
9. fragrance	c. small seedy fruit, coffee bean
10. ship	d. sensation of taste and smell
11. blossom	e. any sort of drink
12. flavor	f. a flower, expecially on a fruit tree
13. destination	g. mix together
14. blend	h. a place to which somebody is going

III. Fill each blank with one of the words given below.

for	over	by	of	in	with	from

15. Coffee beans are picked by hand, one (   ) one.
16. Coffee has been a part of people's cultures (   ) thousand of years.
17. Large coffee farms were started, and coffee was sent all (   ) the world.
18. The berries change (   ) green to dark red in about six months.

19. The beans are packaged (   ) air-tight cans and bags.
20. The tables are full (   ) students drinking their favorite kind of coffee.

IV. Read the following statements and write T if it is true ; write F if it is false.

21. The goats ate coffee berries before man did. (   )
22. Coffee spread from America to Europe. (   )
23. Different countries prefer different blends. (   )
24. Coffee beans are picked by machine. (   )
25. Coffee blossoms are pink color. (   )

V. Choose the word or phrase that best completes each sentence. Change the form of the verbs if necessary.

awake	ship	to	dark	keep

26. Coffee beans are __________ all over the world.
27. Coffee spread from Africa __________ Arabia.
28. That night the goats stayed __________ late.

29. The beans are packaged in air-tight cans to __________ the coffee fresh.

30. In Turkey and Arabia __________ coffee is preferred.

English Reading Treasures

7

Three Humorous Stories

English Reading Treasures 7

Three Humorous Stories

1. The Absent-minded Bishop

A very absent-minded[1)] Bishop was once traveling by train in the district under his care.[2)] When the train stopped at a certain station, the ticket-collector came for the tickets.[3)] The Bishop tried to find his, but could not.

"Never mind, my lord," said the ticket-collector, who knew him well, "I'll come round again when our train arrives at the next station."

---

1) absent-minded : so lost in thought as not to pay attention to what is going around one. 멍하고 있는, 정신나간.

2) care : supervision ; protection. 돌봄, 보호.

3) came for the tickets : = came to check the tickets. 표 검사를 하러 오다.

But at the next station there was the same difficulty : the Bishop could not find his ticket anywhere.

"Don't bother about it ; it really doesn't matter," said the ticket-collector kindly.

"No, no, I must find it," said the Bishop, turning his pockets inside out[4] as he spoke. Finally he confessed, "I want to know where I am going."

2. Too Great a Majority

Geroge Bernard Shaw's[5] gift, of ready wit is world-famous. It is well illustrated by the following story, which tells how he turned the laugh against[6] a man who was expressing disapproval of one of his plays.

It was the first night of "Arms and the Man," a play which was received with much enthusiasm in a crowded house.

4) turn one's pockets inside out : 호주머니 안쪽을 뒤집다.

5) Geroge Bernard Shaw (1856~1950) : Irish-born English dramatist, critic and essayist. (아일랜드 태생의) 영국 극작가 · 비평가.

6) turn the laugh against~ : 야유를 멋있게 ~에게 받아넘기다.

When the curtain fell at the end of the last act, there was tremendous applause and people called[7] eagerly for the author to appear. One man in the gallery[8], however, kept jeering[9] and whistling, thus expressing his disapproval.

Shaw appeared before the curtain, and waited in silence until the applause had died down. Then, looking up at the hostile critic, he said :

"I quite agree with you, sir, but what can we two do against all these people?"

---

7) call : ask. 요청하다.

8) gallery : the highest upper floor in a theater. 맨 위층 관람석, 관객.

9) jeer : make fun of in a rude manner. 조롱하다, 조소하다, 놀리다.

3. The Precious Bowl

An antiquarian[10] who was looking for ancient objects in the houses of the peasants in Normandy one day discovered a charming blue bowl that looked very old. The bowl was lying on the ground and a cat was drinking milk from it.

In order not to attract the attention of the peasant to the value of the bowl, the antiquarian said to him in a casual voice : "What a charming cat you have!" "Yes," said the other. "It's a pretty animal." "Won't you sell it to me?"

"How much would you give me for it?" "Twenty frances. Would it be enough?"

After a few moments, the peasant accepted the offer. The

10) antiquarian : a person who studies, collects or sells old and valuable objects. 골동품 애호가.

antiquarian put twenty frances in the hand of the seller, took the cat on one of his arms and turned toward the gate. But there he stopped suddenly and said to the peasant :

"My poor cat will certainly feel thirsty on the way. May I take the bowl so that the cat may have milk whenever he feels like it?"

But the peasant replied.

"I'm sorry, but I cannot give it to you. Thanks to[11)] this bowl, I have already sold fourteen cats."

11) thanks to : ~ 때문에(=owing to), ~덕택에.

Exercises

I. Read the following paragraph and answer the questions.

(1)An antiquarian who was looking for ancient objects in the houses of the peasants in Normandy one day discovered a charming blue bowl that looked very old. The bowl was lying on the ground and a cat was drinking milk from it. (2)In order not to attract the attention of the peasant to the value of the bowl, the antiquarian said to him in a casual voice :

"What a charming cat you have!" "Yes," said the other. "It's a pretty animal."

"Won't you sell it to me?" "How much would you give me for it?"

"Twenty francs. Would it be enough?"

1. What was an antiquarian looking for?
2. What's the meaning of (1)?
3. What did he discover one day?
4. Which was the one that antiquarian was interested in, bowl or cat?
5. Translate (2) into Korean.

II. Fill each blank with one of the words given below.

for	out	by	so	with

6. A Bishop was traveling ( ) train in his district.
7. An antiquarian was looking ( ) ancient objects.
8. The Bishop turned his pockets inside ( ) as he spoke.
9. I quite agree ( ) you, sir.
10. May I take the bowl ( ) that the cat may have milk.

III. Match the words with the corresponding definitions.

11. jeer	a. the highest upper floor in the theater
12. antiquarian	b. owing to
13. gallery	c. supervision, protection
14. care	d. a person who studies, collects or sells old and valuable objects
15. thanks to	e. make fun of in a rude manner

IV. Read the following statements and write T if it is true ; write F if it is false.

16. The Bishop was absent-minded. (   )
17. Bernard Shaw was angry at the man who expressed his disapproval. (   )
18. Bernard Shaw has the gift of ready wit. (   )
19. The Bishop knew where he was going. (   )
20. The antiquarian paid much more for the cat than its worth. (   )

V. Choose the word or phrase that best completes each sentence. Change the form of the verbs if necessary.

applause	mind	bother	keep	thanks

21. "Never __________, my Lord" said the ticket collector.
22. There was tremendous __________ when the curtain fell.
23. __________ to this bowl, I have sold fourteen cats.
24. Don't __________ about it : it really doesn't matter.
25. One man in the gallery __________ jeering, thus expressing his disapproval.

English Reading Treasures

8

Vegetarians

English Reading Treasures 8

Vegetarians

Some of 10 million Americans today consider themselves to be practicing[1)] vegetarians[2)], according to a Time magazine poll. An additional 20 million have tried vegetarianism sometime in their past. According to a recent survey[3)] by the British government, about 7 percent of the British population see themselves as vegetarians.

However, you cannot

1) practice : v. to do something regularly or as a habit. 반복하여 연습하다, 습관으로 하다.
2) vegetarian : n. a person who eats only or mostly plant foods. 채식자.
3) survey : n. an investigation of the opinions, behaviour, etc. of a particular group of people. 표본조사.

simply put people in one vegetarian category[4]. Vegetarians have many reasons for their lifestyle choices. Some vegetarians adopt[5] their lifestyle for health reasons. Some chose to be vegetarian because of religious or moral[6] causes.

There are also many subgroups among vegetarians when it comes to their diet pattern. Three of them are most typical[7]. The first group is actually not vegetarian by strict definition, although they often call themselves vegetarians. They eat fish but no meat. The second group is lacto-ovo vegetarians, which account for the majority[8] of the vegetarian population. Lacto stands for milk while

---

4) category : n. a group or type of something. 범주, 부문.

5) adopt : v. to accept a practice, custom or habit. 채택하다.

6) moral : adj. related to what is right or wrong. 도덕의.

7) typical : adj. having the usual qualities or features of a particular type of person, thing or group. 전형적인.

8) majority : n. a number or group that is more than half, but not all. 대부분, 과반수.

ovo means eggs. So as you can guess by now, these people include milk and other dairy[9] products in their diet. The third group is called vegan. This type of strict vegetarians gives up any product or food produced from animals. They do not eat animal flesh such as meat, poultry, fish or shellfish nor do they eat animal products such as eggs and milk. Vegans do not eat even honey because bees could be killed during its production. Their diet consists totally of vegetables, vegetable oils and seeds. There are even more extreme vegetarians including people who focus on eating sprouts, and people who live only on fruit, but they are still a small minority[10] among vegetarians.

Vegetarians say that the traditional meat diet can cause all kinds of illness including heart disease and cancer. However, research shows that sometimes a vegetarian diet can bring with it health problems as well. It is sometimes very hard to get important

9) dairy : n. a building in which cows are kept and milked. 착유장.

10) minority : n. a number or group that is less than half of the total. 소수.

nutrients[11)] such as protein and calcium from a non-meat based diet. Extreme vegetarians often experience such symptoms as a fragile bone structure and hair loss.

Vegetarians also insist that meat-eating can affect[12)] your brain and even your personality, sometimes making you cruel and mean. They say that when animals are killed, they generate a lot of stress hormones, which affect humans who consume their meat.

But if you look at some famous vegetarians in history, that belief is somewhat questionable. Maximilien Robespierre was a vegetarian and he ordered thousands of people to be killed during the French Revolution. Adolf Hitler was also a strict vegetarian yet he is infamous[13)] for his murderous and hateful personality. George Bernard Shaw was a vegetarian but there's no evidence to show that his diet ever quieted his trademark cynicism[14)].

– From *Reading for Everyday Life*

11) nutrient : n. a substance contained in food that is essential to life. 영양분.

12) affect : v. have an effect on. ~에 영향을 미치다.

13) infamous : adj. well known for being bad or evil. 악명높은.

14) cynicism : n. the attitude, beliefs or behaviour of a cynic. 냉소.

Exercises

I. Read the following paragraph and answer the questions.

The second group is lacto-ovo vegetarians, which account for the majority of the vegetarian population. Lacto stands for milk while ovo means eggs. So as you can guess by now, these people include milk and other dairy products in their diet. The third group is called vegan. (1)This type of strict vegetarians gives up any product or food produced from animals.

1. What kind of group takes the majority of the vegetarian population?
2. What does lacto mean?
3. Which group drink milk and eat dairy products?
4. What is the third vegetarian group called?
5. Translate (1) into Korean.

II. Fill each blank with one of the words given below.

up	as	to	by	for

6. Vegetarians have many reasons ( ) their lifestyle choices.
7. There are also many subgroups among vegetarians when it comes ( ) their diet pattern.
8. So as you can guess ( ) now, these people include milk and other dairy products in their diet.
9. This type of strict vegetarians gives ( ) any product or food produced from animals.
10. It is sometimes very hard to get important nutrients such ( ) protein and calcium from a non-meat based diet.

III. Match the word or expression with its definition.

11. practice	a. well known for being bad or evil
12. category	b. to accept a practice, custom or habit
13. adopt	c. have an effect on
14. affect	d. a group or type of something
15. infamous	e. to do something regularly or as a habit
16. extreme	f. to show a strong opinion

IV. Choose the closest meaning to the following words.

17. strict

    a. stubborn b. stern c. specific d. special

18. account

    a. agree b. consider c. explain d. present

19. generate

    a. analyze b. continue c. operate d. produce

20. research

    a. study b. question c. answer d. homework

V. Mark each sentence as either true(T) or false(F) according to the text.

21. The majority of the British population sees themselves as vegetarians. (   )
22. People practice vegetarianism for diverse causes. (   )
23. There are more vegans than lacto-ovo vegetarians in the world. (   )
24. Vegetarians tend to gain more weight than meat eaters. (   )
25. Some vegetarians think a diet affects one's personality. (   )

English Reading Treasures

9

Raising Royal Treasures

English Reading Treasures
9

Raising Royal Treasures

Bit by bit, divers are recovering pieces of Cleopatra's lost palace

It's a tale full if romance, sneaky[1] tricks, tragedy and, most of all, girl power. On top of that, it's true. The real-Life story of Cleopatra, a beautiful 17-year-old girl when she became the powerful ruler of ancient Egypt, has fascinated people for thousands of years. Dozens of plays, books and movies have told of her quest for power and love. Now new information about Cleopatra's life is coming to the surface. Parts of her ancient royal court have been found near Alexandria, Egypt - under water!

---

1) sneaky : a. behaving in a secret and sometimes dishonest or unpleasant way. 비열한.

Finding a Lost Island

Ancient Egyptian writings and drawings show that Cleopatra owned a royal palace on an island named Antirhodos. The island was near Alexandria, the capital city of Egypt during Cleopatra's reign in the first century B.C. Although the city of Alexandria still exists today, floods and earthquakes buried Antirhodos under water more than 1,600 years ago. But it wasn't lost for good. In 1996 undersea explorer Franck Goddio found it beneath just 18 feet of water, off the shore of Alexandria. The ruins of what appears to be

Cleopatra's palace lay buried in layers of mud seaweed and garbage.

Goddio and his team of divers have spent two years uncovering statues, columns, pavement and pottery that may have belonged to the young queen. Their work is sponsored in part by the Discovery Channel, which will broadcast a television special on the new findings.

Among the most sensational finds are two statues of sphinxes, imaginary creatures with the head of a human and the body of a lion. The faces of the sphinxes are in surprisingly good shape. So good, that experts have been able to identify one face as that of King Ptolemy XII, Cleopatra's father.

How does it feel to come face to face underwater with an ancient sphinx? "It's fascinating!" Goddio says. "You see the sphinx, and it's looking at you. You know that it's the father of Cleopatra and that Cleopatra once saw it. It's like a dream."

One Queen, Two Love Stories

Cleopatra and her brother Ptolemy XIII began to rule Egypt together in 51 B.C. In keeping with royal custom, the brother and sister were married! But Ptolemy did not want to share the throne, and he forced Cleopatra out of the palace.

During this time, another great civilization was rising to power in Rome. Its main leader, Julius Caesar, traveled to Egypt. In order to meet with him, Cleopatra is said to have sneaked[2)] into the palace rolled up in a carpet!

Caesar soon fell in love with Cleopatra. He helped her push Ptolemy aside and take control of Egypt. Romans were angered by Caesar's ties with Egypt's queen. Some feared that he had grown too powerful. Four years after meeting Cleopatra, Caesar was murdered by his enemies.

Three years passed before a new Roman leader, Mark Antony, met Cleopatra. Just like Caesar before him, Antony fell in love with her. He moved into Cleopatra's palace at Antirhodos. Soon people back in Rome feared that Antony was more interested in Egypt than in his own empire. They turned against him and Egypt. In despair, Cleopatra and Antony took their own lives. Ancient Egypt's last queen died at the age of 39. Soon after her death, the Romans took control of Egypt.

2) sneak : v. to go somewhere secretly, trying to avoid being seen. 살금살금 들어오다.

Though her reign ended 2,000 years ago, Cleopatra continues to enchant people everywhere. For that reason, Goddio hopes to set up an underwater museum at the palace site. Visitors would be able to experience Cleopatra's world up close. "To be there, underwater where she reigned and died." says Goddio, "is unbelievable."

An Ancient Treasure Trove[3)]

The Phoenicians were the great seafarers of the ancient world. Their ships sailed the Mediterranean 5,000 years ago, when the Egyptians were building the pyramids. Later they traded with the ancient Greeks. Their home base was in what is now Lebanon, but they set up colonies in North Africa and Spain. Their ships sailed as far as England, carrying such goods as glass, cedarwood[4)], wine and purple dye[5)] to trade.

---

3) Treasure Trove : valuable things that are found hidden and whose owner is unknown. 매장물.

4) cedarwood : u. the hard red wood of the cedar tree, that has a sweet smell. 삼나무.

5) dye : u. a substance made from plants or chemicals which is mixed into a liquid and used to change the colour of something such as cloth or hair. 염색, 염색하다.

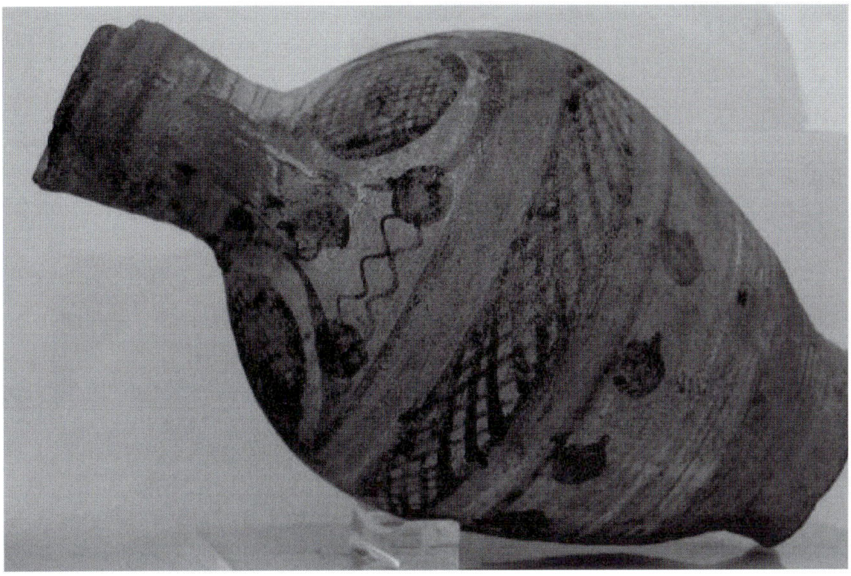

Though they are mentioned in the Bible and other ancient texts, we know little of these long ago sailors. That's why historians were overjoyed last month with the discovery of what looks like a sunken Phoenician ship. It was found nearly 3,000 feet deep in the Mediterranean. Pictures taken by a robot submarine show clay pots made in a style used by Phoenicians 2,500 years ago. Such pots, called amphoras, were used to carry wine, oil and other goods. "It's an incredible find," says Greg Stemm, of Odyssey Marine Exploration, which made the discovery. He hopes to raise[6] money to explore the wreck and look for other treasures.

6) raise : v. to bring or collect money or people together. 조달하다, 마련하다.

Did You know?

-Cleopatra (69 B.C.~30 B.C.)

Queen of Egypt, one of the great romantic heroines of all time. Her name was widely used in the Ptolemaic family ; there were many earlier Cleopatras. The daughter of Ptolemy XI, she was married at the age of 17 (as was the family custom) to her younger brother Ptolemy XII. The force and character of the royal pair was, however, concentrated in the alluring[7)] (though apparently not beautiful) and ambitious queen. She led a revolt against her brother, and, obtaining the aid of Julius Caesar, she won the kingdom, although it remained a vassal[8)] of Rome. Her young brother-husband was accidentally drowned in the Nile. She then married her still younger brother Ptolemy XIII, but she was the mistress of Caesar and followed him to Rome ; there she bore a son, Caesarion (later Ptolemy XIV), who

7) alluring : a. attractive and exciting in a mysterious way. 유혹하는.

8) vassal : a country that depends on and is controlled by another country. 속국, 종속.

was said to be his. Returning to Egypt after the murder of Caesar, she was visited (42B.C.) by Mark Antony. He fell hopelessly in love with her, and Cleopatra, conscious of her royalty and even her claims to divinity as the pharaoh's daughter, seems to have hoped to use Antony to reestablish the real power of the Egyptian throne. They were married in 36 B.C. Most of the Romans feared and hated Cleopatra, and Octavian (later Augustus) undertook to destroy the two lovers. Antony and Cleopatra were defeated off Actium in 31 B.C., and, returning to Alexandria, they tried to defend themselves in Egypt. When they failed, Antony committed suicide by falling on his sword. Cleopatra, faced by the cold and unmoved Octavian, also killed herself. Her schemes failed, but her ambition, capability, and remarkable charm have left a great impression on history. Shakespeare's *Antony and Cleopatra*, based on Plutarch, describes the tragic end of the queen's career, and Dryden's *All for Love* : or, *The World Well Lost* is reworking of Shakespeare. *Caesar and Cleopatra,* the comedy by G.B. Shaw, deals with the early years of her history.

– From *Topics for In-depth Reading*, Time - H&B Press, 2007

Exercises

I. Read the following paragraph and answer the questions.

(1)Ancient Egyptian writings and drawings show that Cleopatra owned a royal palace on an island named Antirhodos. The island was near Alexandria, the capital city of Egypt during Cleopatra's reign in the first century B.C. Although the city of Alexandria still exists today, floods and earth quakes buried Antirhodos under water more than 1,600 years ago. (2)But it wasn't lost for good.

1. What is the name of the island where Cleopatra's palace located?
2. What had happened to Cleopatra's palace?
3. What is the capital city of Egypt?
4. Translate (1) into Korean.
5. Translate (2) into Korean.

II. Match the words with the corresponding definitions.

6. treasure trove	a. to bring or collect money together
7. broadcast	b. attractive in a mysterious way
8. dye	c. a country that depends on another country
9. sneak	d. unknown owner's hidden valuable things
10. alluring	e. a substance for changing the color of things
11. raise	f. to send out programs on television or radio
12. vassal	g. to go somewhere secretly, unseen

III. Read the following statements and write T if it is true ; write F if it is False.

13. Cleopatra's palace was historically burnt down in a terrible fire. (   )
14. One face of the two statues of sphinxes are identical to Cleopatra's mother. (   )
15. Both Caesar and Anthony fell in love with Cleopatra at first sight. (   )
16. The Phoenicians were the great farmers of the ancient world. (   )

IV. Fill each blank with one of the prepositions given below.

ago	to	with	into	by	beneath	at

17. Undersea explorer found it (   ) just 18 feet of water.
18. You see the sphinx and it is looking (   ) you.
19. Cleopatra is said to have sneaked (   ) the palace.
20. Last month historians were overjoyed (   ) the discovery.
21. Anthony committed suicide (   ) falling on his sword.
22. Their ships sailed the Mediterranean 5,000 years (   ).
23. Their work is sponsored in part (   ) the Discovery channel.

V. Fill each blank with one of the verbs given below. Change the form of the verbs if necessary.

close	dye	raise	drown
broadcast	used	charm	

24. Her remarkable __________ have left a great impression on history.
25. Their ships contain such goods like glass, wine and purple __________.
26. Greg wants to __________ money to explore the wreck.

27. OCN Channel will _________ a television special on the new movies.
28. Visitors can explore and experience Cleopatra's world up _________.
29. Such pots, called amphoras, were _________ to carry wine, oil and other goods.
30. Her young brother-husband was accidentally _________ in the Nile.

English Reading Treasures

10

The Meaning of Color

English Reading Treasures 10

The Meaning of Color

Cultures vary in many ways and one of the ways in which they differ from[1] each other is in their use of color, especially in clothing. In many Western countries, for instance, a bride wears white, and the white of her gown represents purity. If a bride were to wear any bright colors at all, it would be considered strange indeed. In Korea, however, white represents mourning and the bride who wears the

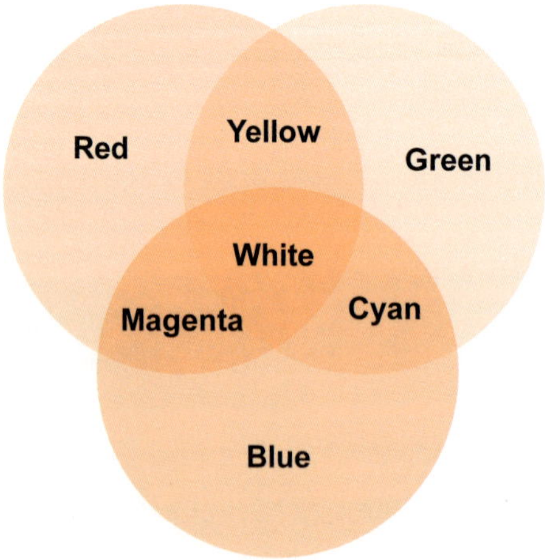

1) differ from : ~와 ~는 다르다(= is different from).

traditional bridal clothing of the country wears bright colors and not white.

In the matter of the color for mourning there is again a great difference between the West and Korea, for in the Western world the color for mourning is black, quite the opposite of the white worn in Korea. Besides this, there is much use in modern times for dark colors in the West, for men's clothing is usually made in dark colors.

Again, Korea differs from the West in that the young Korean man is free to[2] wear lovely bright colors and rich fabrics if he wears the traditional clothes of his country. What a contrast there is between the bridegrooms of such countries as the United States and Great Britain and the bridegrooms of Korea when Korean bridegrooms wear their traditional grab! Were they to stand side by side, the Korean would look rather like a handsome peacock while the Western bridegroom would look a good deal like a penguin. Gray is a color largely reserved for the elderly in Korea while in the West a little girl, a little boy, a young man, or a young woman will be very pleased to have a new gray suit in spring. It is true, though, that for young people on both sides of the world, clothes are usually of bright happy colors.

The Korean primary school child goes to school dressed in bright reds, yellows, greens, and blues just as do his fellow students on

2) free to : 마음대로 ~할 수 있다.

the other side of the world. The big difference is that while Korean students begin to wear uniforms which are dark in color when they enter middle school, few children in the Western world wear uniforms. Instead they continue to wear the bright colors they wore they were younger.

The foreigner, when he first sees Korean farmers, is surprised to see that they have chosen white as the color for their work clothes since the farmers of the Western world usually wear dark clothes, usually very dark blue or brown. It must be difficult for the Korean farm housewife to take care of her husband's clothes. The mud stains that get onto white clothes in a Korean rice field are surely difficult to clean off.[3)]

The farmer's white shoes are quite a different matter though. His white shoes look nice indeed, and because they are made of rubber they are easy to clean. His shoes are far easier to care for than are the Western farmer's shoes, for the latter are likely to be of leather. Leather is hard to clean and when it gets wet in the fields it gets stiff and then the farmer's shoes hurt his feet.

In one other matter at least, East and West agree in their use of color for clothing. In a city like Seoul, when spring comes, the ladies appear on the streets in clothes of lovely pastel, flowerlike colors, and around on the other side of the world their sisters also begin in spring to wear clothes in soft, pale shades quite different from the darker, stronger colors of winter clothing.

3) clean off : 씻어내다, 지워버리다.

Exercises

I. Read the following paragraph and answer the questions.

Korean farmers have chosen white as the color for their (1)working clothes. (2)The mud stains that get onto white clothes in a field are surely difficult to clean off. It must be difficult for the Korean farm housewife to take care of her husband's clothes. But the farmer's white shoes look nice indeed. Because (3)they are made of rubber that they are easy to clean.

1. What color have Korean farmers chosen for their working clothes?
2. Translate (1) into Korean.
3. What is the meaning of (2)the mud stains?
4. What does (3)they refer to?
5. What are the Korean farmer's shoes made of?

II. Fill in the blanks with the proper words below.

by	off	between	in	at	from

6. There is a great difference ( ) the West and Korean.
7. Cultures vary ( ) many ways.
8. Were they to stand side ( ) side, the Korean would look like a handsome peacock.
9. In one other matter ( ) least, East and West agree in their use of color for clothing.
10. In spring, ladies wear in soft, pale shades quite different ( ) the darker, strong colors of winter clothing.
11. The mud stains that get onto white clothes are surely difficult to clean ( ).

III. Match each word with the best meaning.

12. fabric	a. the state of being pure or clean
13. purity	b. weeping over one's death
14. mourning	c. hard, firm, tight, or solid
15. pale	d. on the other side, the furthest way
16. stiff	e. very light color or almost white
17. opposite	f. cloth or texture

IV. Read the following statements and write T if it is true, write F if it is false.

18. In Korea a bride wears white which represents mourning. (   )
19. In the Western world black color represents mourning exactly same as in Korea. (   )
20. Every young Western man is free to wear pastel colors when they wear the traditional clothes. (   )
21. Korean bridegroom looks rather like peacock because of his traditional clothing. (   )
22. Most of primary school children in the world dress in bright colors. (   )
23. In the Western gray is reserved for young people in spring. (   )

V. Circle the letter of the word that best completes the sentence.

24. French __________ from English in many respects.

    a. differ   b. differs

    c. is differed   d. different

25. There is a great __________ between the West and Korea.

    a. differ   b. differed

    c. difference   d. different

26. "left" is __________ to "right."

a. oppose b. opponent

c. opposite d. oppressive

27. A Korean man can wear bright colors clothing _________ he wears the traditional clothes.

a. if b. between

c. though d. instead

28. _________ we take the bus, it will be cheaper.

a. Were b. If

c. When d. Though

29. _________ I not busy, I would accept your invitation.

a. Were b. Was

c. Am d. If

30. Uniforms are reserved for the teens in Korea _________ in the West they wear the gray colors.

a. while b. for

c. between d. if

English Reading Treasures

11

Michelangelo

English Reading Treasures 11

Michelangelo

They say that the border line between genius and insanity is a thin, thin line and few geniuses can live their whole life without occasionally crossing over to the side of insanity. Michelangelo[1)] was one of those few.

Michelangelo was a contemporary[2)] of all the great men of the Italian Renaissance. He knew and worked with da Vinci, Raphael, Lorenzo de' Medici, Julius II and outlived[3)] them all. He was a sculptor, painter, a bronze caster[4)], and architect,

1) Michelangelo, Buonarroti (1475~1564) : Italian sculptor, painter and architect. 미켈란젤로(이탈리아 화가, 조각가, 건축가).

2) contemporary : n. a person living in the same period as. 같은 시대의 사람.

3) outlive : v. live longer than. ~보다 더 오래살다.

4) caster : n. a person forming (metal, plastic etc.) into a particular shape by pouring or pressing into a mold. 주조자, 주물공(鑄物工).

and engineer, a stone cutter. Only Leonardo da Vinci surpassed him in the variety of his talents. But this is precisely what is amazing in the life of Michelangelo. Da Vinci fully intended to be everything that he became. Michelangelo never wanted to be a painter, a bronze caster, an architect, or an engineer. He was first and foremost[5] a sculptor. He loved the feel of the hammer and chisel in his hands. He worked mainly in marble. He said that stone was alive, that it contained in itself the forms he wanted to sculpture, that it was his job to draw those forms out of the living stone.

It seemed that marble was Michelangelo's life. He lived to sculpture. He sculptured to live. When he began a piece of work, he would sculpture for days on end[6] almost without eating, drinking, or sleeping. At such times he would not even bother to change his clothes, but would take his few hours' sleep dressed as he was. As he hammered away at his block of marble, his hair would become white with dust. The white powder would cake[7] around his eyes and his nose. He became almost unrecognizable, and then it was easy for someone to say that he had crossed over the border into insanity.

---

5) first and foremost : above all else ; most importantly. 가장 중요하게, 무엇보다도 먼저.

6) on end : continuously. 계속하여.

7) cake : v. form into a hard mass. 뭉쳐지다, 덩어리지다.

There were other times, too, when someone might say Michelangelo was insane. His father was a completely untalented merchant, incapable of earning a cent. His brothers were also untalented, and greedy too. In spite of all the money that Michelangelo earned, he gave it all to support his relatives and lived most of his life in poverty. He had a quick temper[8] and a sharp

8) quick temper : tendency to become quickly angry. 급한 성미.

tongue[9]. He even insulted the popes, and one day he so angered Julius II that the Pope stuck Michelangelo with his cane. In those days, when the Pope was a king as well as a religious leader, this seemed to be the height[10] of insanity. Michelangelo lived to be 90, and although he became friends with many excellent women, he never married.

However, Michelangelo remained a genius and never crossed the border line. When he sculptured and painted, he forgot about his personal appearance because in those moments only one thing was important to him - to express in stone or color the thoughts of beauty that he held in his head. He lived in poverty because he loved his family and could not refuse their requests, even when those requests were stupid. He never married because he could not take himself from his work to tie himself to a family. Even the popes, who could not have put him

9) have a sharp tongue : use severe, sharp or harshly critical language. 말이 신랄한.
10) height : the highest limit ; extreme. 절정, 극치.

in prison many times for his insults, never punished him because they understood that Michelangelo's sharp tongue came from his devotion to art and beauty.

All Michelangelo's other talents were developed of necessity[11], only because he wanted to sculpture. He made bronze statue of Pope Julius and painted the Sistine Chapel[12] so that the Pope would give him money to buy marble. He became an engineer and rebuilt the walls of Florence, the city where he was born, to protect it from enemies, so that he could have time to sculpture. He became the

11) of necessity : necessarily ; inevitably. 필연적으로.

12) Sistine Chapel : the principal chapel in the Vatican at Rome. 시스틴 성당.

architect of the church of St. Peter in Rome because the first architect wanted to tear down[13] the Sistine Chapel with Michelangelo' frescos.

Sculpturing was Michelangelo's consolation, his recreation, his joy. When he was angry he sculptured. When he was sad he sculptured. When he was happy he sculptured. And he created the greatest masterpieces[14] of sculpture the world has ever seen. No one will ever be able to surpass his Pieta[15], his David, or his Moses. Speaking of the Sistine Chapel, Leonardo da Vinci told Michelangelo, "You have painted too well. Your human figures are perfect. Future painters will try to surpass you, but they will not succeed. You have left nothing to surpass[16]."

13) tear down : v. wreck or demolish. (건물 등을) 헐다, 해체하다.

14) masterpieces : n. an extremely skilful piece of work, especially the greatest work of an artist or writer. 대작, 걸작.

15) Pieta : a representation in painting, sculpture, of Mary the mother, grieving over the body of Christ after the Crucifixion. 피에타(성모 마리아가 그리스도의 시체를 무릎에 안고 슬퍼하는 그림[상]).

16) surpass : v. to do or be better than sb/sth. ~보다 낫다, 능가하다.

Exercises

I. Read the following paragraph and answer the questions.

He made bronze statue of Pope Julius and painted the Sistine Chapel so that the Pope would give him money to buy marble. He became an engineer and rebuilt the walls of Florence, the city where he was born, to protect it from enemies, so that he could have time to sculpture. He became the architect of the church of St. Peter in Rome because the first architect wanted to (1)tear down the Sistine Chapel with Michelangelo' frescos. (2)Sculpturing was Michelangelo's consolation, his recreation, his joy.

1. Why did he make bronze statue and painted the Chapel?
2. What did he do to protect the Florence?
3. Where was he born?
4. What is the reason for his becoming the architect of the church of St. Peter?
5. How do you pronounce (1)tear down?
6. Translate (2) into Korean.

II. Fill each blank with one of the words given below.

down	for	away	in	between	of

7. They say that the border line (   ) genius and insanity is a thin, thin line.
8. When he began a piece of work, he would sculpture (   ) days on end almost without eating, drinking, or sleeping.
9. As he hammered (   ) at his block of marble, his hair would become white with dust.
10. His father was a completely untalented merchant, incapable (   ) earning a cent.
11. He lived (   ) poverty because he loved his family and could not refuse their requests.
12. The first architect wanted to tear (   ) the Sistine Chapel with Michelangelo' frescos.

III. Match the word or expression with its definition.

13. outlive	a. demolish
14. first and foremost	b. extreme
15. cake	c. form into a hard mass
16. tear down	d. continuously

17. surpass	e. most importantly
18. on end	f. to do or better than
19. height	g. live longer than

IV. Mark each sentence as either true(T) or false(F) according to the text.

20. Leonardo Da Vinci outlived Michelangelo. (   )
21. The only thing important to Michelangelo when he sculptured and painted was his appearance. (   )
22. Michelangelo's father was a successful businessman. (   )
23. Michelangelo was married and had a large family. (   )
24. Popes never punished him for his insults because they understood that those came from his devotion to art and beauty. (   )
25. Leonardo Da Vinci said that Sistine Chapel is a great masterpiece that no one could surpass it. (   )

English Reading Treasures

12

'Starbucks' and 'Subway'

English Reading Treasures
12

'Starbucks' and 'Subway'

- They Did It Their Way

Starbucks and Subway are American companies. They share a lot in common. They are two of the best-known and most successful businesses in the food and beverage[1] industry. Their brands have become household names in America. They grew at a time when there was a lot of competition from companies that were already in business for a long time. They have shown impressive profit[2] margins[3] in an industry where margins historically are tight and competition is extremely fierce. They have successfully extended to international markets such as Korea, Japan and India.

However, each company also represents a different business model from the other. Of course one sells coffee and the other sells sandwiches as its core product. But beyond that, their road to success diverges[4] at one key point. While Starbucks has kept its now more than 8,000 chain stores corporate-owned[5], Subway has built its empire through franchised[6] stores. In fact, Subway keeps only one

1) beverage : any sort of drink. 마실 것, 음료.
2) profit : an amount of money that you gain when you are paid more for something than it cost you to make, get, or do it. 이익, 이득.
3) margin : the difference between two amounts, especially the difference in the number of votes or points between the winner and the loser in an election or other contest. 여백, 여유, 매매차익금, 이익.
4) diverge : the first thing becomes different from the second or develops differently from it. You can also say that two things. 분기하다, 갈라지다.
5) corporate-owned : 법인이 소유하는.
6) franchise : an authority that is given by an organization to someone, allowing them to sell its goods or services or to take part in an activity which the organization controls. 특권, 참정권.

company-owned store. These two business models have their own advantages and challenges. Keeping chain stores corporate-owned allows the company to make quick decisions in reaction to changing market situations. It also enables the company to open new store locations without making its franchise store owners worry about losing their share of profits due to more competition. The corporate-owned store business model also enables a company to maintain a consistent corporate identity throughout its network of stores.

Franchising, on the other hand, is a business model in which the company sells its business formula - store design, food recipe, supplies - to independent individuals. It has several apparent advantages. First, franchising is an easy way for the company to get access to capital because the company uses other people's money to grow. As long as the product and the system are attractive to customers, you can open new outlets[7)] in a lot of strategic locations all at the same time. It also encourages a strong sense of ownership among franchises who invest in their own stores. Franchises often freely express their opinions on how to improve their profitability[8)] and headquarters often adopts the best ideas from among them.

The two business models are different in many aspects. One's

7) outlet : a shop or organization which sells the goods made by a particular manufacturer. 소매점.

8) profitability : yielding profit. 수익성.

advantage easily becomes the other's disadvantage. But Starbucks and Subway have shown that both models can be very successful, as long as you do either well. Starting as a small coffee importer in Seattle, Starbucks now runs more than 8,000 outlets worldwide. Founded in 1965 with $1,000 that the founder borrowed from a bank, Subway opened its 18,000th store in 2003. The chain now has more outlets in the United States than McDonald's.

– From *Reading for Everyday Life*

Exercises

I. Read the following paragraph and answer the questions.

The two business models are different in many aspects. One's advantage easily becomes the other's disadvantage. But Starbucks and Subway have shown that both models can be very successful, (1)as long as you do either well. Starting as a small coffee importer in Seattle, Starbucks now runs more than 8,000 (2)outlets worldwide. Founded in 1965 with $1,000 that the founder borrowed from a bank, Subway opened its 18,000th store in 2003. The chain now has more outlets in the United States than McDonald's.

1. Are Starbucks and Subway same in many aspects?
2. When was Starbucks opened?
3. Did Starbucks start as a big fancy coffee shop?
4. What's the meaning of (2)?
5. Translate (1) into Korean.

II. Fill each blank with one of the words given below.

other	at	of	as	to

6. There was a lot (   ) competition from companies.
7. They have extended to international markets such (   ) Korea and India.
8. Of course one sells coffee and the (   ) sells sandwiches.
9. You can open new outlets all (   ) the same time.
10. Store owners don't worry about losing their share of profits due (   ) more competition.

III. Match the words with the corresponding definitions.

11. diverge — a. any sort of drink
12. profitability — b. the first thing becomes different the second
13. beverage — c. yielding profit
14. franchise — d. difference between two amounts
15. margin — e. an authority that is given by an organization to someone

IV. Read the following statements and write T if it is true ; write F if it is false.

16. Starbucks has kept now more than 6,000 chain stores. ( )
17. Coffee is core product of Subway. ( )
18. Starbucks started its business in Seattle. ( )
19. Starbucks has its headquarters in Japan. ( )
20. McDonald's has more outlets in the United States than Subway's. ( )

V. Choose the word or phrase that best completes each sentence.

as long as	adopted	bottom	road	independent

21. He is financially __________ of his parents.
22. I am not sure if making money is the __________ to happiness.
23. The company has __________ a new pension system for its employees.
24. Banking is a business of trust at the __________.
25. __________ the store is open, we can buy some milk.

VI. Circle the letter of the word that best completes the sentence.

26. Franchising is a business model in which the company sells its business ________ .

    a. policy b. fund c. plan d. formula

27. Subway opened the 18000th store in ________.

    a. 2008 b. 1965 c. 2000 d. 2003

28. Franchises often freely express their opinions on how to improve their ________.

    a. profitability b. product
    c. business d. circumstances

29. Starbucks and Subway are two of the best known and most successful businesses in the ____________ industry.

    a. food and steak b. coffee and steak
    c. food and beverage d. coffee and soup

30. As long as the product and the system are __________ to customers, they can open an new outlet at any place.

    a. attentive b. wonderful
    c. effective d. attractive

English Reading Treasures

13

Hobbies

English Reading Treasures

13

Hobbies

One of the main reasons people have hobbies is to kill time. Many of the great developments in science and technology have given us all a lot of time beyond that which we fill with necessary activity. But few of us use that extra time creatively, so we get bored. So we need a hobby to make the time pass enjoyably : we collect stamps or learn how to cook or just listen to our CDs.

One of the problems, though, is with having expensive hobbies.

Usually they are intended to show off our wealth or our being up-to-date[1] with some supposed trend, rather than supporting any genuine interest. Too often, we can't really afford it ; but even if we can, we just feed[2] our general discontent because we are spending a lot of money but not reliving our boredom.

Having a hobby is supposed to be an enjoyable way to relax. On weekends or at night, too many people have no interest in going anywhere or doing anything, so they just stay at home watching TV or nagging[3] their families. But if they could develop an interest in something else, they would be too absorbed in[4] it to bother the other people at home. Domestic tranquility[5] would

1) up-to-date : based on the latest information, changes, improvement, or styles. 최신의.
2) feed : nourish. 먹이를 주다, 기르다.
3) nag : bother or annoy. 성가시게 잔소리하다.
4) absorbed in : completely interested in. 열중한, 몰두한.
5) tranquility : calmness. 평온, 고요함.

be achieved! Even better would be something the entire family could enjoy together. A fun, stimulating, inexpensive hobby would help keep the family close and comfortable with each other.

I'm happy whenever I meet someone who shares my interests. We usually become friends right away because we often have similar characteristics. We can immediately understand each other, and we have something vital to talk about. In fact, talking itself is one of the greatest hobbies we can enjoy, don't you think so? And it's certainly one of the least expensive - is that what people mean when they say "talk is cheap"?

Exercises

I. Read the following paragraph and answer the questions.

One of the main reasons people have hobbies is (1)to kill time. Many of the great developments in science and technology have given us all a lot of time beyond that which we fill with necessary activity. But few of us use that extra time creatively, so we get bored. So we need a hobby to make the time pass enjoyably : we collect stamps or learn how to cook or just listen to our CDs.

1. What are the two reasons given for having hobbies?
2. Why are the hobbies necessary in the modern world?
3. Why do we get bored?
4. What does (1) mean?
5. What kinds of hobbies are given in the paragraph?

II. Fill each blank with one of the words given below.

about	off	with	of	in

6. Usually they are intended to show (   ) our wealth or our being up-to-date with some supposed trend.
7. They would be too absorbed (   ) it to bother the other people at home.
8. A fun, stimulating, inexpensive hobby would help keep the family close and comfortable (   ) each other.
9. We can immediately understand each other, and we have something vital to talk (   ).
10. In fact, talking itself is one (   ) the greatest hobbies we can enjoy.

III. Match the words or expression with its definition.

11. up-to-date	a. nourish
12. feed	b. bother or annoy
13. nag	c. calmness
14. feed	d. completely interested in
15. tranquility	e. based on the latest information

IV. Mark each sentence as either true(T) or false(F) according to the text.

16. If we use our extra time creatively, we don't need a hobby. (   )
17. One of the problems of having expensive hobby is to show off one's wealth. (   )
18. Domestic tranquility can be achieved by having a hobby. (   )
19. A fun stimulating hobby for the entire family could bring them close to each other. (   )
20. We tend to make friends easily when we talk about other than hobbies. (   )

V. Choose the word or phrase that best completes each sentence. Change the form of the verbs if necessary.

at	share	enjoyably	get	enjoyable

21. Few of us use that extra time creatively, so that we _________ bored.
22. We need a hobby to make the time pass _________.
23. Having a hobby is supposed to be an _________ way to relax.
24. They just stay _________ home watching TV or nagging their families.
25. I'm happy whenever I meet someone who _________ my interests.

English Reading Treasures

14

Mother

English Reading Treasures 14

Mother

My mom and I sat in the small college cafe with large mugs of something that smelled like lemon and tasted like home. We were catching up on[1] the past four months of our lives and the hours just weren't long enough. Sure, we had talked on the phone and occasionally[2] written. But the calls were long distance, and it was rare to find a moment when my roommate wasn't for the phone or my younger brother or sister wasn't waiting for my mom. So while we knew of each other's experiences, we had not yet dissected[3] them. As we discussed her knew job, and my latest paper, my new love, and her latest interview, I leaned back into my cushion and thought : I always knew when she became my mother, but when had she become my friend?

As far back as I can remember my mom was always the first

1) catch up on : to find out about things that have happened. ~된 것에 대해 알다.

2) occasionally : now and then or here and there ; at times ; from time to time. 가끔, 때때로.

3) dissect : to cut up a dead body, a plant, etc. in order to study it. 해부하다.

that I came to with every tear and every laugh. When I lost a tooth and when I found a friend, when I fell from my bike, and when I got back on it, she was there. She never judged me ; she let me set my own expectations[4]. She was proud when I succeeded and supportive[5] when I didn't.

She always listened ; she seemed to know when I was asking for advice and when I just needed a good cry. She multiplied[6] my excitement with her own and divided[7] my frustrations[8] with her empathy[9] and understanding. When she picked me up from school, she always asked about my day. And I remember one day asking about hers. I think

4) expectation : That which is expected ; the object of expectance ; a thing expected or looked forward to. 기대.
5) supportive : giving help, encouragement or sympathy. 협력적인, 따뜻하게 대하는.
6) multiply : to combine by multiplication. 곱하다, 증가시키다.
7) divide : to separate or make something separate into parts. 나누다.
8) frustration : the feeling of being frustrated. 좌절.
9) empathy : the ability to imagine and share another person's feelings, experience, etc. 감정이입.

I was a little surprised that she had so much to say. We rarely had late night talks (because she was already asleep), nor early morning ones[10)](because I was not yet up), but in between the busy hours of our filled days, we found the time to fill each other's ears with stories and hearts with love. She slowly shared more and more of her own life with me, and that made me feel more open[11)] with her. We shared experiences and hopes, frustrations and fears.

Learning that she still had blocks to build and to tumble[12)] made me more comfortable with my own. She made me feel that my opinions were never immature[13)] and my thoughts never silly. What surprises me now is not that she always remembered to tell me "sweet dream", but that she never forgot to tell me that she believed in me. When she started going through some changes in her life, I had the opportunity to tell her that I believed in her too.

My mother had always been a friend. She had given me her heart in its entirety ;[14)] but her soul, she divulged[15)] in pieces, when she

10) ones : talks. 대화.

11) open : willing to talk ; honest ; frank. 자발적인 얘기, 진실된.

12) Learning that she still had blocks to build and to tumble : 어머니에게 여전히 만들고 넘어뜨려야 할 장애물이 있음을 아는 것.

13) immature : not sensible in behaviour or in controlling one's feelings ; less mature than one would expect. 미숙한.

14) entirety : the state of being entire or complete in its entirety. 전체, 상태가 전체가 되는.

15) divulge : to make something known, esp. a secret. 공개하다, 폭로하다.

knew that I was ready.

I sat across from the woman who had given me my life and then shared hers with me. Our mugs were empty, but our hearts were full. We both knew that tomorrow she'd return to the bustle[16] of Los Angeles and I'd remain in the hustle[17] of New Haven. I know that we are both growing and learning. Yet, we continue to learn about each other and grow closer. Our relationship was like the tea we had sipped,[18] mixed with honey and lemon ; the longer it steeped,[19] the better it tasted.

16) bustle : excited, intense and noisy activity. 야단법석, 소란.

17) hustle : the busy movement of and activity of man people together. 매우 서두름.

18) sip : to drink something, taking a very small amount each time. 조금씩 마시다.

19) steep : to put food in a liquid and leave it there for some time, esp. to soften it or give it flavor. 액체에 적시다.

Exercises

I. Read the following paragraph and answer the questions.

(1)As far back as I can remember my mom was always the first that I came to with every tear and every laugh. When I lost a tooth and when I found a friend, when I fell from my bike, and when I got back on it, she was there. She never judged me ; she let me set my own expectations. She was proud when I succeeded and supportive when I didn't. She always listened ; she seemed to know when I was asking for advice and (2)when I just needed a good cry.

1. Did her mother always judge her?
2. Who was the first that she came to with every tear and laugh?
3. What's the meaning of (1)?
4. Who was there when she lost a tooth and fell from her bike?
5. Translate (2) into Korean.

II. Fill each blank with one of the word given below.

up	through	for	in	with

6. She seemed to know when I was asking (   ) advice.
7. We were catching (   ) on the past four months of our lives.
8. She started going (   ) some changes in her life.
9. I sat across from the woman who shared her life (   ) me.
10. (   ) between the busy hours of our days, we found the time to talk.

III. Match the words with the corresponding definitions.

11. mug	a. giving help, encouragement or sympathy
12. dissect	b. a fairly large cup for drinking from
13. empathy	c. to cut up a dead body, a plant, etc.
14. frustration	d. the ability to imagine and share other person's feelings
15. supportive	e. a feeling of being frustrated
16. entirety	f. to make something known, esp. a secret
17. immature	g. in its complete form, as a whole

18. divulge	h. excited, intense and noisy activity
19. bustle	i. not sensible in behaviour

IV. Read the following statements and write T if it is true ; write F if it is false.

20. They sat in the Starbucks coffee shop with their large mugs. ( )
21. They had no chance to talk on the phone at all before they met. ( )
22. Her mother still had blocks to build and to tumble. ( )
23. They had late night talk often. ( )
24. Her mother lives in Los Angeles. ( )
25. "Sweet dreams" was the encouraging word of her mother. ( )

V. Translate the following sentence and explain it as much as you can.

The longer it steeped, the better it tasted.

English Reading Treasures

15

English Poems

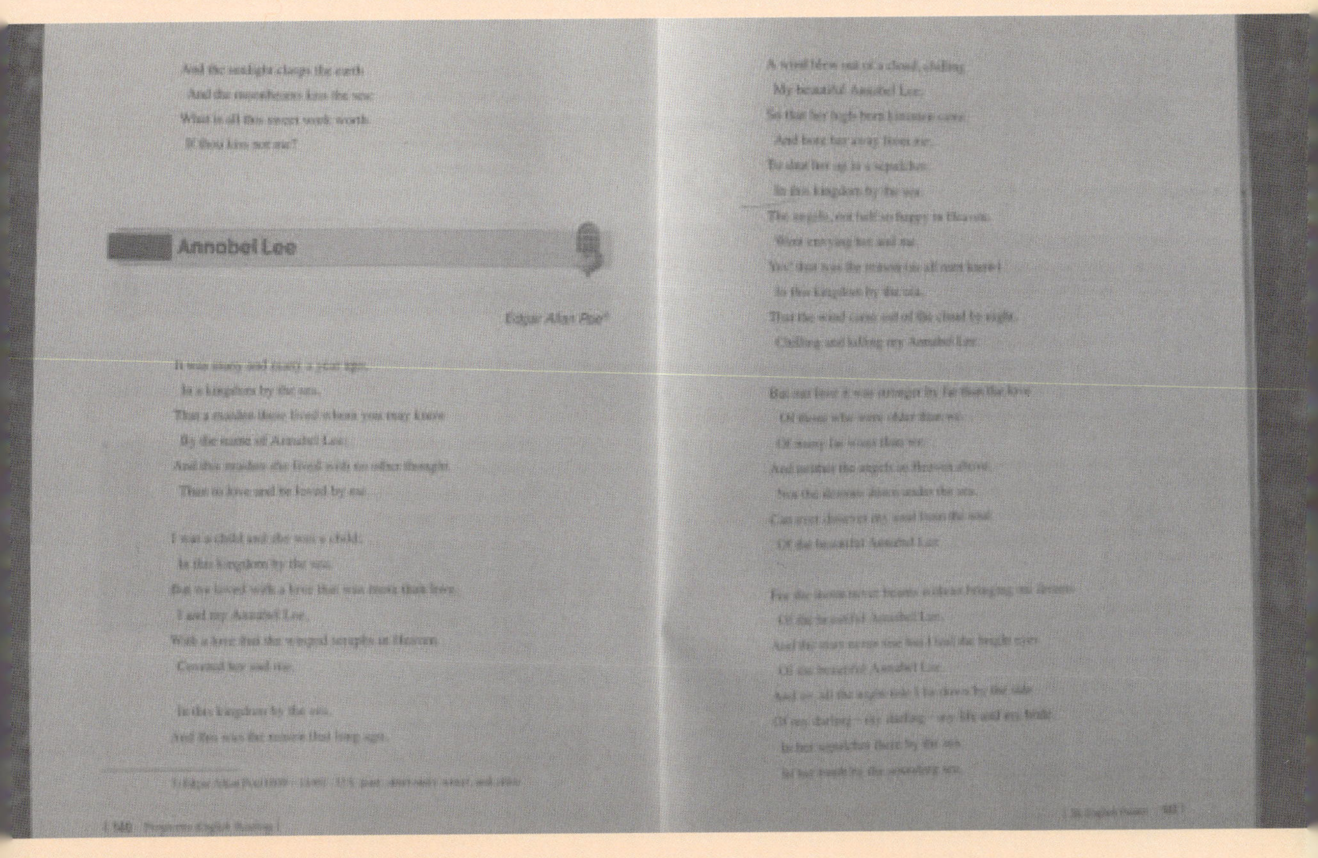

English Reading Treasures 15

English Poems

My Heart Leaps Up

William Wordsworth[1)]

My heart leaps[2)] up when I behold
A rainbow in the sky :
So was it when my life began ;
So is it now I am a man ;
So be it when I shall grow old,
Or let me die!
The child is father of the Man ;
And I could wish my days to be
Bound each to each by natural piety.

1) William Wordsworth (1770~1850) : 영국 낭만주의의 계관시인.

2) leap : jump high in the air or jump a long distance. (높이) 뛰다.

Daffodils[3)]

William Wordsworth

I wandered lonely as a cloud
That floats on high o'er vales[4)] and hills,
When all at once I saw a crowd,
A host, of golden daffodils ;
Beside the lake, beneath the trees,
Fluttering and dancing in the breeze.

Continuous as the stars that shine
And twinkle on the Milky Way,[5)]
They stretched in never-ending line
Along the margin of a bay :

3) daffodil : a yellow spring flower with a central part shaped like a tube and a long stem. 수선화.

4) vale : a valley. 계곡, 골짜기.

5) Milky Way : the pale strip of light consisting of many stars that you can see stretched across the sky at night. 은하수.

Ten thousand saw I at a glance,
Tossing their heads in sprightly dance.

The waves beside them danced, but they
Out-did the sparkling[6] waves in glee :
A poet could not but be gay,
In such a jocund[7] company :
I gazed - and gazed - but little thought
What wealth the show to me had brought :

6) sparkle : clear and bright and shines with a lot of very small points of light. 불꽃, 번쩍임.

7) jocund : cheerful. 유쾌한, 즐거운.

For oft, when on my couch I lie
In vacant or in pensive mood,
They flash upon that inward eye
Which is the bliss of solitude ;
And then my heart with pleasure fills,
And dances with the daffodils.

Annabel Lee

Edgar Allan Poe[8)]

It was many and many a year ago,
In a kingdom by the sea,
That a maiden there lived whom you may know
By the name of Annabel Lee ;
And this maiden she lived with no other thought
Than to love and be loved by me.

I was a child and she was a child ;
In this kingdom by the sea ;
But we loved with a love that was more than love,
I and my Annabel Lee,
With a love that the winged seraphs[9)] in Heaven
Coveted her and me.

8) Edgar Allan Poe (1809~1849) : 미국의 시인 · 단편작가, 비평가.

9) seraph : a kind of angel. 천사.

In this kingdom by the sea,
And this was the reason that long ago,
A wind blew out of a cloud, chilling.
My beautiful Annabel Lee ;
So that her high-born kinsmen came,
And bore her away from me,
To shut her up in a sepulcher[10],
In this kingdom by the sea.
The angels, not half so happy in Heaven.
Went envying her and me.
Yes! that was the reason (as all men know)

10) sepulcher : grave, tomb. 무덤.

In this kingdom by the sea,
That the wind came out of the cloud by night,
Chilling and killing my Annabel Lee.

But our love it was stronger by far than the love
Of those who were older than we,
Of many far wiser than we ;
And neither the angels in Heaven above,
Nor the demons down under the sea,

Can ever dissever[11] my soul from the soul

11) dissever : divide. 분리하다, 나누다.

Of the beautiful Annabel Lee.

For the moon never beams without bringing me dreams
Of the beautiful Annabel Lee,
And the stars never rise but I feel the bright eyes
Of the beautiful Annabel Lee.
And so, all the night-tide I lie down by the side
Of my darling - my darling - my life and my bride,
In her sepulcher there by the sea,
In her tomb by the sounding sea.

Stopping by Woods on a Snowy Evening

Robert Frost[12)]

Whose woods these are I know.
His house is in the village though ;
He will not see me stopping here
To watch his woods fill up with snow
My little horse must think it queer

12) Robert Frost (1874~1963) : 미국의 시인.

To stop without a farmhouse near
Between the woods and frozen lake
The darkest evening of the year.

He gives his harness[13)] bells a shake
To ask if there is some mistake.
The only other sound's the sweep
Of easy wind and downy flake.[14)]

The woods are lovely, dark and deep.
But I have promises to keep,
And miles to go before I sleep,
And miles to go before I sleep.

13) harness : a set of strips of leather and metal pieces that is put around a horse's head and body so that the horse can be controlled and fastened to a carriage, etc. 방울.

14) flake : a small thin piece of something. 눈송이.

English Reading Treasures

16

The Gift of Understanding

English Reading Treasures 16

The Gift of Understanding

Paul Villiard[1)]

I must have been about four years old when I first entered Mr. Wigden's sweet shop, but the smell of that wonderful world of penny treasures[2)] still comes back to me clearly more than half a

1) Paul Villiard (1910~1974) : 미국의 아동문학가.

2) penny treasures : 싸구려 사탕들.

century later. Whenever he heard tiny tinkle the bell attached to the front door, Mr. Wigden quietly appeared to take his stand[3] behind the counter. He was very old, and his head was topped with a cloud of fine, snow-white hair.

Mother went into town once or twice a week, and, since in those days baby-sitters were almost unheard-of[4], I usually accompanied her. It became a regular routine for her to take me into the sweet shop for some special treat, and after that first visit I was always allowed to make my own choice.

I knew nothing of money at that time. I would watch my mother hand something to people, who would then hand her a package or a bag, and slowly the idea of exchange came into my mind. Sometime about then I reached a decision. I would journey the interminable[5] two streets to Mr. Wigden's all alone. I remember the tinkle[6] of the bell as I managed, after some considered effort, to push open the big door. Enthralled[7], I walked my way slowly down the display counter.

---

3) take his stand : 자리잡고 서다.
4) unheard of : adj. that has never been known or done. 전례가 없는, 금시초문의.
5) interminable : adj. continuing for too long and therefore boring or annoying ; endless. 끝없는, 지루하게 긴.
6) tinkle : n. a light ringing sound. 딸랑딸랑거리는 소리.
7) enthral : v. to keep someone completely interested ; to facinate. ~의 마음을 사로잡다.

When I had picked out a promising assortment, Mr. Wigden leaned over and asked. "You have the money to pay for all these?" "Oh, yes," I replied, "I have lots of money," I reached out my fist, and into Mr. Widgen's open hand I dumped half-dozen cherry seeds carefully wrapped in silver tinfoil. Mr. Widgen stood gazing at the palm of his hand ; then he looked searchingly at me for a long moment.

"Isn't it enough?" I asked him anxiously. He sighed gently. "I think it is a bit too much," he answered. "You have some change coming." He walked over to his old-fashioned cash register and cranked open the drawer[8]. Returning to the counter, he leaned over

8) drawer : n. a part of a piece of furniture such as a desk, used for keeping things in. 서랍.

and dropped two pennies into my outstretched hand.

My mother scolded[9] me about taking the trip alone when she found me out. I don't think it ever occurred to her to ask about the financial arrangement. I was simply cautioned not to go again unless I asked first. I must have obeyed, and evidently, when permission was granted[10] for me to make the trip, a cent or two was given me for my purchases, since I don't remember using cherry seeds a second time. In fact, the whole affair, insignificant[11] to me then, was soon forgotten in the busy occupation of growing up.

When I was six or seven years old my family moved east, where I grew up, eventually married and established my own family. My wife and I opened a shop where we bred and sold exotic[12] fish. The aquarium trade was then still in its infancy, and most of the fish were imported from Asia, Africa and South America. Few species sold for less then five dollars a pair.

---

9) scold : v. to speak angrily to sb, especially a child, because they have done sth wrong ; reprimand. 꾸짖다.

10) grant : v. to give or allow someone something, usually in an official way. 주다, 승인하다.

11) insignificant : adj. not big or valuable enough to be considered important ; meaningless. 대수롭지 않은.

12) exotic : adj. from or in another country, especially a tropical one ; foreign. 이국적인.

One sunny afternoon a little girl came in accompanied[13)] by her brother. They were perhaps five and six years old. I was busy cleaning the tanks. The two children stood with wide, round eyes, staring at the jeweled beauties[14)] swimming in the crystal-clear water. "Gosh," exclaimed the boy, "Can we buy some?" "Yes," I replied. "If you can pay for them." "Oh, we have lots of money", the little girl said confidently.

Something in the way she spoke gave me an odd feeling of familiarity. After watching the fish for some time they asked me for pairs of several different kinds, pointing them out as they walked

13) accompany : v. to travel or go somewhere with somebody ; go with somebody. 동반하다.

14) jeweled beauties : jewel fish. 열대어 종류의 물고기.

down the row of tanks. I netted their choices into a travelling container and slipped it into an insulated bag for transport, handing it to the boy. "Carry it carefully," I cautioned.

He nodded and turned to his sister. "You pay him," he said. I held out my hand, and as her clenched fist approached me I suddenly knew exactly what was going to happen, even what the little girl was going to say. Her fist opened, and into my outstretched palm she dumped two nickels and a dime.

At that instant I sensed the full impact of the legacy[15)] Mr. Wigden had given me so many years before. Only now did I recognize the challenge I had presented to the old man, and realize how wonderfully he had met it.

I seemed to be standing again in the little sweet shop as I looked at the coins in my own hand. I understood the innocence of the two children and the power to preserve[16)] or destroy[17)] that innocence, as Mr. Wigden had understood those long years ago. I was so filled up with the remembering that my throat ached. The little girls was standing expectantly before me. "Isn't it enough?" she asked in a small voice.

15) legacy : n. money or property that you receive from someone after they die. 유산.

16) preserve : v. to keep a particular quality, feature, etc. ; to keep. 보존하다.

17) destroy : v. to damage sth so badly that it no longer exists, works ; devastate. 파괴하다.

"It's a little too much," I managed to say over the lump in my throat. "You've got some change to come." I rummaged[18] round in the cash drawer, dropped two cents into her open hand, then stood in the doorway watching the children walk away, carefully carrying their treasure.

When I went back into the shop, my wife was standing on a stool with her arms submerged to the elbow in a tank where she was rearranging the plants. "What was that all about?" she asked. "Do you know how many fish you gave them?" "About 30 dollars' worth," I answered, the lump still in my throat. "But I couldn't have

18) rummage : v. to search for something by moving things around carelessly and looking into, under and behind them. 뒤지다.

done anything else."

When I had finished telling her about old Mr. Wigden, her eyes were wet, and she stepped off the stool and gave me a gentle kiss on the check. "I still smell the gumdrops," I sighed, and I'm certain I heard old Mr. Wigden chuckle[19] over my shoulder as I swabbed[20] down the last tank.

– From *The Gift of Understanding* by Paul Villiard

19) chuckle : v. to laugh quietly. 싱글싱글 웃다.

20) swab : v. to wash a surface, especially the open flat areas, with a wet cloth or mop. 걸레질하다, 훔치다.

Exercises

I. Read the following paragraph and answer the questions.

I must have been about four years old when I first entered Mr. Wigden's sweet shop, but the smell of that wonderful world of penny treasures still comes back to me clearly more than half a century later. Whenever he heard the tiny tinkle the bell attached to the front door, Mr. Wigden quietly appeared to take his stand behind the counter. He was very old, and his head was topped with a cloud of fine, snow-white hair. Mother went into town once or twice a week, and, since in those days baby-sitters were almost unheard-of, I usually accompanied her.

1. What did they sell at Mr. Wigden's sweet shop?
2. How many years is half a century?
3. When does Mr. Wigden take his stand behind the counter?
4. What does Mr. Wigden look like?
5. How often mother goes into town?
6. Why did mother bring him whenever she goes into town?

II. Fill each blank with one of the words given below.

at	of	out	over	with

7. His head was topped (   ) a cloud of fine, snow-white hair.
8. I knew nothing (   ) money at that time.
9. When I had picked (   ) a promising assortment, Mr. Wigden leaned over and asked.
10. Then he looked searchingly (   ) me for a long moment.
11. Returning to the counter, he leaned (   ) and dropped two pennies into my outstretched hand.

III. Match the word or expression with its definition.

12. unheard of	a. a group of different types of something
13. tinkle	b. to wash a surface, with a wet cloth or mop
14. assortment	c. to search for something by moving things around carelessly
15. rummage	d. that has never been known or done
16. swab	e. a light ringing sound
17. scold	f. reprimand

IV. Choose the correct answer for each question.

18. As a little boy, the narrator was much attracted by _______________.

    a. the tinkling of Mr. Wigden's front door bell

    b. the various kinds of candies at Mr. Wigden's shop

    c. the colorful decorations of Mr. Wigden's shop

    d. Mr. Wigden's personality

19. When the narrator told Mr. Wigden that he had "lots of money," he _______.

    a. understood very well the idea of exchange

    b. had already learned how to purchase things in a shop

    c. meant to deceive the old man

    d. thought anything valuable to him could be used as money

20. Mr. Wigden gave the narrator some change, because _________________.

    a. the payment was a bit too much

    b. he didn't want to humiliate the narrator

    c. he wanted to make fun of the narrator

    d. he pretended to accept the narrator's money willingly

21. The narrator's mother scolded him about going to Mr. Wigden's alone, probably because ______.

    a. she knew he hadn't paid for the candies

b. she worried about his safety

c. candies were no good for his health

d. Mr. Wigden wouldn't be happy to see him in his shop again

V. Mark each sentence as either true(T) or false(F) according to the text.

22. The narrator hadn't sensed the full impact of Mr. Wigden's legacy until the same kind of situation confronted him. ( )
23. The narrator has lost a lot of money by giving away a lot of fish to small children. ( )
24. Mr. Wigden's legacy to the narrator was a loving heart to protect children's innocence. ( )
25. The two children has given a cherry seed to pay for the tropical fish. ( )

English Reading Treasures

17

Travel Can Broaden the Mind

English Reading Treasures 17

Travel Can Broaden the Mind

Many people have the idea that travel broadens[1] the mind. This means that if you stay in your own country the whole time, your ideas remain narrow. Whereas, if you travel, you see new customs, eat new foods, meet new people, and come back home with a broader outlook[2].

But does this always - or even usually-happen? A friend of mine who lives in England and had never been outside it until last summer decided to go over to France for a trip. When he returned, I asked him how he liked it. "Terrible," was his answer. "I couldn't get a nice cup of tea anywhere. Thank goodness I'm back."

I asked him whether he hadn't had any good food while he was

1) broaden : v. to be come wider, to increase your experience, knowledge, etc. 넓히다.

2) outlook : n. the attitude to life and the world of particular person, group or culture. 시야, 견해.

there. "Oh, the dinners were all right, I found a little place where they made good fish and chips. They were passable[3], though they were not as good as ours. But the breakfasts were terrible : no bacon or kippers or haddocks. I had fried eggs and chips, but it was quite a business[4] getting them to make them."

I was surprised at his ignorance[5] of French breakfasts, but he did not appear to notice that. "They expected me to eat rolls," he went

3) passable : a. fairly good but not excellent satisfactory. 웬만한, 쓸 만한.

4) quite a business : = quite a difficult task. 꽤 힘든 일.

5) ignorance : n. a lack of knowledge or information about something. 무지함.

on, "and when I asked for marmalade, they brought strawberry jam instead. Mind you[6], they insisted that it was marmalade! The trouble is they don't know English."

I thought it useless to explain that we borrowed the word 'marmalade' from French, and that it means, in that language, any kind of jam. So I said, "But didn't you eat any of the famous French food?" "What? Me?" he said. "Of course not. Give me good old English food every time! None of those fancy bits[7] for me!"

He had gone to France to pass his fortnight's[8] vacation. He had expected to stay at a hotel near Tours[9], with occasional outings to enjoy a magnificent[10] view over the Loire valley or to visit the famous castles dating from the Middle Ages. He didn't say a word about them, nor did I feel like asking what he had seen. He had returned with a prejudice against life in France. Obviously his mind had not been broadened by travel.

He had been so simple as to expect that he could live in France exactly as if he were in England. And so, everything French had been judged strictly from his own English viewpoint. This does not,

---

6) mind you : take this fast into account. 주의를 기울이다.

7) fancy bits : n. bits (of food) higher than real value extravagant bit. 가격이 터무니없이 비싼 음식.

8) fortnight : two weeks. 2주.

9) Tours : n. a city in the west central France, on the river Loire. 프랑스 서부 도시.

10) magnificent : adj. extremely attractive and impressive. 장려한, 수려한.

of course, happen only to Englishmen in France. All over the world, people can be found judging what they see, hear, taste, and smell according to their own habits and customs.

It might be said, after all, that the ideal for the traveler is to try to be acceptable as an outsider in certain respects but not in all. He should not try to be somebody else. However, he should have the advantages of getting the foreign people to show him a generous attitude. He can expect to get by with ignorance about small things by reason of being an outsider. He must learn, those details of correct conduct of the foreign country which are considered as a matter of course by its people.

Every society has areas of behavior where one has to conform without argument. Such behavior usually cannot be freely discussed in the society. Other areas of behavior are regarded[11] as less important matters and can be made a topic for discussion. All this should be learned in your classes in social studies and foreign languages.

Today, as foreign travel is more popular, everyone should learn to find its value for educational purposes. Travel broadens the mind if one is well trained for it.

11) regard : v. to think about sb/sth. in a particular way. ~으로 여기다.

Exercises

I. Read the following paragraph and answer the questions.

A friend of mine who lives in England and had never been outside it until last summer decided to go over to France for a trip. When he returned, (1)I asked him how he liked it. "Terrible," was his answer. "I couldn't get a nice cup of tea anywhere. Thank goodness I'm back." I asked him whether he hadn't had any good food while he was there. "Oh, the dinners were all right, I found a little place where they made good fish and chips. They were passable, though they were not as good as ours.

1. Where does the author's friend live?
2. When did the he visit France?
3. Was he happy to be back in England?
4. While he stayed in France what did he have for dinner?
5. Translate (1) into Korean.
6. Was French fish and chips better than English fish and chips?

II. Fill each blank with one of the words given below.

from	as	at	for	of

7. I couldn't get a nice cup (   ) tea anywhere.
8. They were passable, though they were not as good (   ) ours.
9. I was surprised (   ) his ignorance of French breakfasts.
10. When I asked (   ) marmalade, they brought strawberry jam instead.
11. I thought it useless to explain that we borrowed the word 'marmalade' (   ) French.

III. Match the word or expression with its definition.

12. after all	a. to become wider, to increase your experience, knowledge, etc.
13. haddocks	b. the attitude to life and the world of a particular person, group or culture
14. outsider	c. in conclusion
15. outlook	d. a sea fish like a cod
16. broaden	e. a person who is not accepted as a member of a society, group, etc.

IV. Choose the closest meaning to the following words.

17. broaden

    a. cardboard
    b. to increase your experience
    c. to hold
    d. wide

18. passable

    a. excellent satisfactory
    b. fairly good
    c. passing
    d. passive

19. ignorance

    a. avoidance
    b. neglect
    c. a lack of information
    d. attention

20. magnificent

    a. bigger
    b. extremely attractive
    c. attractiveness
    d. magically

21. prejudice

    a. insufficient knowledge
    b. hostility
    c. pride
    d. a biased opinion

V. Choose the word or phrase that best completes each sentence.

expand	educational	broaden	travel	cultures	judging

22. __________ is one of the greatest ways to __________ the mind.
23. Travel teaches you about other people, __________, ways of life.
24. It also teaches you about yourself and helps to __________ your narrow world perspective.
25. All over the world, people can be found __________ what they see, hear, taste, and smell according to their own habits and customs.
26. As foreign travel is more popular, everyone should learn to find its value for __________ purposes.

VI. Mark each sentence as either true(T) or false(F) according to the text.

27. Few people agree that travelling abroad can broaden the mind. ( )
28. Travel enlarges the mind, if it is taken in the right spirit. ( )
29. Travelling experience helps you to confirm your prejudice against life in other countries. ( )
30. The author's friend thinks France is a wonderful place to visit. ( )

English Reading Treasures

18

The Necklace

English Reading Treasures 18

The Necklace

Guy de Maupassant[1)]

1

She was one those pretty and charming[2)] girls, born by chance in a lower-middle class family. And she allowed herself to marry a clerk in the Ministry of Education. She suffered from the poorness of her house, from its mean[3)] walls, worn[4)] chairs, and ugly curtains. All these things, which other women of her class would not

1) Guy de Maupassant (1850~1893) : 프랑스의 소설가.
2) charming : adj. very pleasant or attractive. 매력적인.
3) mean : adj. poor and dirty in appearance ; cheap. 초라한.
4) worn : adj. haggard with weariness. 닳아 해진.

even noticed, were pain and grief to her.

One evening her husband came home with a smile on his face, holding a large envelope in his hand. "Here's something for you," he cried. She tore the paper and drew out a printed card on which were these words : *The Minister of Education and Madame Ramponneau request the pleasure of the company of Monsieur and Madame Loisel at the Ministry on the evening of Monday, January the 18th.*

Instead of being delighted, as her husband hoped, she threw the invitation down on the table, saying : "What's the good of this to me?" "Why, darling, I thought you'd be pleased. You never go out, and this is a great occasion. I had great difficulty in getting it. You'll see all the really big people there."

She looked at him with anger and said impatiently : "What do you think I'm to wear?" He had not thought about it ; he said : "Why, the dress you go to the theatre in. I think it's charming. He stopped, quite at a loss[5] when he saw that his wife was beginning to cry. "What's the matter?" he said. "I'm quite miserable at not having any jewels to wear," she replied. "I shall look very poor. I'd rather not go to the party." "Wear flower," he said. "They're very smart at this time of year. For ten francs you could get two or three magnificent[6] roses." She was not convinced. "No, there's nothing so

5) at a loss : be embarrassed. 당황하다.

6) magnificent : adj. extremely attractive and impressive ; superb. 굉장히 좋은.

humiliating[7] as looking poor in the middle of a lot of rich women."

"How stupid you are!" cried her husband. "Go and see your friend, Madame Forestier, and ask her to lend you some jewels. You know her quite well enough to do that." She uttered[8] a cry of delight[9] : "That's a good idea! I never thought of it."

The next day she went to see her friend and told her of her trouble, Madame Forestier took out a large box, brought it to Madame Loisel, opened it, and said : "Take what you like, my dear."

First she saw a pearl necklace, then suddenly she found in a black case a magnificent diamond necklace ; her heart began to beat. Her hands trembled as she lifted it. She put it round her neck, upon her dress. Then, with hesitation, she asked : "Could you lend me this, just this alone?" "Yes, of course." She threw her arms round her friend's neck, kissed her with delight, and went away with the necklace.

The day of the party arrived. Madame Loisel had a triumph[10].

7) humiliating : adj. feeling ashamed and lose the respect of other people ; undignified. 굴욕적인.

8) utter : v. to say something. 말하다.

9) delight : n. a feeling of great pleasure. 기쁨.

10) triumph : n. a great success, achievement or victory. 승리.

She was the prettiest woman in the room, elegant, graceful smiling, and quite happy. All men looked at her, asked her name, and wanted to be introduced to her. All of them wanted to dance with her. The Minister himself noticed her. She danced madly, drunk with delight, thinking of noting in the triumph of her beauty, in the pride of her success.

She left about four o'clock in the morning. Her husband threw over her shoulders the garments he had brought for her to go home in, simple everyday clothing, whose poorness was in sharp contrast to the beauty of the ball dress.

She noticed this and was anxious to hurry away, so that she

would not be noticed by the other ladies who had on their costly[11] furs. When they got into the street they could not find a cab ; they began to look for one, They walked down towards the Seine, shivering. At last they found one, which brought them to their door. It was the end, for her. As for him, he was thinking that he must be at the office at ten next morning. She took off the garments[12], standing in front of the mirror to see herself once more in all her glory.

2

"What's the matter with you?" asked her husband, already half undressed. She turned to him in distress[13] ; "Madame Forestier's necklace has gone!" He jumped up. "What! It's impossible!" They searched in the folds[14] of her

11) costly : adj. expensive. 값비싼.

12) garment : n. a piece of clothing. 의복.

13) distress : n. a feeling of great worry or unhappiness. 고민, 곤란.

14) folds : n. a part of sth, especially cloth, that is folded or hangs as if it had been folded. 주름.

dress, in the pockets, everywhere. They could not find it.

"And you sure that you still had it on when you left the ball?" he asked. "Yes. I touched it in the hall." "But if you had lost it in the street, we should have heard it fall. It must be in the cab." "Yes. it probably is. Do you remember the number of the cab?" "No. You didn't notice it, did you?" "No."

They looked at each other. At last Loisel put on his clothes again. "I'll go back along the way we walked," he said, "and see if I can find it." And he went out. She remained in her evening clothes, without the strength[15] even to go to bed.

Her husband returned about seven. He had found nothing. He went to the police station, to the newspapers to offer a reward[16], to the cab companies, everywhere he thought there was a hope. By the end of a week they had lost all hope. Loisel, who looked five years older, said : "We must do something about replacing the diamonds."

Then they went from jeweller to jeweller, looking for another necklace like the first. At last in a shop they found a diamond necklace which seemed to them exactly like the one lost. Its price was forty thousand francs. They could have it for thirty-six thousand.

Loisel had eighteen thousand francs which his father had left

15) strength : n. the quality of being physically strong. 힘.

16) reward : n. a thing that you are given because you have done sth good. 보상.

him. He borrowed the rest, getting a thousand from one man, five hundred from another, one hundred here, sixty there. He gave notes of hand[17)] on ruinous[18)] terms, going to money-lenders of every kind. He mortgaged[19)] the whole remaining years of his life. Then he went to get the new necklace and put down thirty-six thousand francs upon the jeweller's counter.

When Madame Loisel took the necklace back to Madame Forestier, the latter did not, as her friend had feared, open the case. If she had noticed the change, what would she have thought? What would she have said? Would she not have taken her for a thief?

Madame Loisel came to know the terrible life of poverty. Right from the start she played her part bravely. This terrible debt must be paid. She would pay it. The servant was dismissed. They changed their flat ; they took a

17) a note of hand : n. a promissory note. 증서, 약속어음.

18) ruinous : adj. costing a lot of money and more than you can afford. 터무니없이 비싼.

19) mortgage : v. to give ownership of (property) as security for a loan. 저당잡히다.

garret[20] under the roof.

Every month some notes of hand had to be paid off, others to be renewed to get time. Her husband worked in the evenings keeping a merchant's books, and often at night he did copying at five sous[21] a page. And this life went on for ten years.

At the end of ten years everything was paid off, including the interest and the interest upon interest. Madame Loisel looked old now. She had become like all other strong, hard, rough women of poor households. Her hair was neglected, her hands were red and her voice loud. She even scrubbed[22] floors. But sometimes, when her husband was at the office, she would sit down by the window and think of that evening long ago, of the ball[23] at which she had been so beautiful and so much admired. What would have happened if she had not lost the necklace? Who knows? How strange life is! How little is needed to ruin or to save!

One Sunday, as she had gone for a walk along the Champs-Elysees as a rest after the labours of the week, she suddenly saw a lady who was taking a child out for a walk. It was Madame Forestier, still young, still beautiful, still attractive. Madame Loisel's

20) garret : n. an attic room, often a dingy one. 다락방.

21) sou : n. a French coin of low value. 프랑스 동전.

22) scrub : v. to clean sth by rubbing it hard, perhaps with a brush and usually with soap and water. 닦다, 문지르다.

23) ball : n. a large formal party with dancing. 무도회.

heart began to beat fast. Should she speak to her? Yes, certainly. And now that she had paid, she would tell her all. Why not? She went up to her.

"Good afternoon, Jeanne." The other did not recognize her, and was surprised at being thus familiarly addressed by a poor woman "But... madame... I don't know you must be making a mistake." "No... I'm Mathilde Loisel." Her friend uttered a cry. "Oh!... my poor Mathilde, how you've changed...!"

"Yes, I've had some hard times since I saw you last ; and many sorrows... and all because of you." "Because of me? What do you mean." "You remember the diamond necklace you lent[24)] me for the ball at the Ministry?" "Yes. What about it?" "Well, I lost it." What! You brought it back to me." "I brought you another one exactly like it. And for the last ten years we've been paying for it. You'll understand it hasn't been easy for us ; we had no money... Well, it's paid for at last, and I'm very glad."

Madame Forestier had stopped. "You say you bought a diamond necklace in place of[25)] mine?" "Yes. You hadn't noticed it? They were very much alike." And she smiled. Madame Forestier, deeply moved took her two hands. "Oh, my poor Mathilde! But mine was an

---

24) lend : v. to allow somebody to use sth that belongs to you, which they have to return to you later ; loan. 빌려주다.

25) in place of~ : in stead of ~. ~ 대신에.

imitation[26]. It was worth only five hundred francs at most[27]!"

– From *The Necklace* by Guy de Maupassant

26) imitation : n. a copy of sth, especially sth expensive ; fake. 모조.

27) at most : 기껏해야.

Exercises

I. Read the following paragraph and answer the questions.

Madame Forestier took out a large box, brought it to Madame Loisel, opened it, and said : "Take what you like, my dear." First she saw a pearl necklace, then suddenly she found in a black case a magnificent diamond necklace ; (1)her heart began to beat. Her hands trembled as she lifted it. She put it round her neck, upon her dress. Then, with hesitation, she asked : "Could you lend me this, just this alone?" "Yes, of course."

1. What was in the large box that Madame Forestier opened?
2. What was in the black case?
3. Why did her heart begin to beat? Explain (1).
4. What did she put around her neck?
5. Did Madame Forestier lend her friend a piece of jewel?

II. Fill each blank with one of the words given below.

with	at	for	by	towards	of

6. Instead ( ) being delighted, as her husband hoped, she threw the invitation down on the table.
7. He stopped, quite ( ) a loss when he saw that his wife was beginning to cry.
8. She threw her arms round her friend's neck, kissed her ( ) delight.
9. They walked down ( ) the Seine, shivering.
10. when her husband was at the office, she would sit down ( ) the window and think of that evening long ago.
11. Well, it's paid ( ) at last, and I'm very glad.

III. Match the word or expression with its definition.

12. worn	a. costing a lot of money and more than you can afford
13. at a loss	b. an attic room, often a dingy one
14. distress	c. be embarrassed
15. garret	d. haggard with weariness
16. ruinous	e. a feeling of great worry or unhappiness

IV. Choose the correct answer for each question.

17. What is Madame Loisel's reaction when her husband tells her they have been invited to a party?

    a. She was excited.
    b. She wasn't delighted.
    c. She was happy.
    d. She cried in happiness.

18. What did Madame Forestier lend Loisel?

    a. a pearl necklace
    b. a magnificent dress
    c. a diamond necklace
    d. a cab

19. How long did it take the Loisels to pay off the debt?

    a. 11 years
    b. 12 years
    c. 10 years
    d. 9 years

20. The Loisels bought the diamond necklace for ______________ .

    a. eighteen thousand francs
    b. five hundred francs
    c. forty thousand francs
    d. thirty-six thousand francs

V. Mark each sentences as either true(T) or false(F) according to the text.

21. Madame Loisel wore magnificent roses to the ball. (   )

22. Madame Loisel borrowed a pearl necklace from her rich friend. (   )

23. The necklace was found in the cab. (   )

24. Madame Loisel worked herself weary to repay her debt. (   )

25. Madame Loisel and Madame Forestier are no longer friends. (   )

English Reading Treasures

19

A Hotel with a Difference

English Reading Treasures 19

A Hotel with a Difference

Three Unusual Hotels

The Green Magic Tree House, in India, is the perfect hotel for anybody who likes adventure. Guests must drive for miles through the jungle to find it in the middle of a tea and coffee plantation[1]. There are two tree houses to choose from, one 30 meters and the other 35 meters above the ground. Both houses have two floors. The bedrooms are above a living area and there are bathrooms and showers.

1) plantation : n. a large area of land, especially in a hot country, where crops such as coffee, sugar, rubber, etc. are grown. 대규모 농원.

You can get up to the rooms and move between floors by using ladders[2)]. You can go from one tree house to the other on a rope bridge. The houses sometimes move about in the wind but the views are fantastic.

The Ice Hotel is in Jukkasjarvi, a village in Sweden 200 kilometers north of the Arctic Circle. Every winter, a team of architects, designers and snowbuilders build the hotel. This year there are 80 rooms. Everything is made of ice, which in this part of the world is crystal clear. The walls, the floors, the ceilings, and even the furniture are all made of ice. The beds are made of ice too, but guests sleep on warm reindeer skins. Outside it can be -37 degrees centigrade, so inside it feels quite comfortable. The hotel has a bar,

2) ladder : n. a piece of equipment for climbing up and down a wall. 사다리.

where guest can drink vodka from glasses made of ice. It's very popular-because there isn't much else to do.

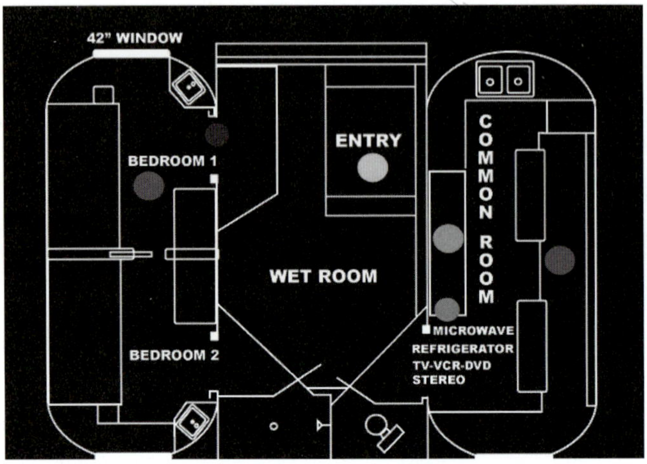

To spend a night at Jules Underwater Lodge[3] in Florida, guests need to scuba dive seven meters under the sea. They enter the lodge through a door at the bottom of the building. Inside, the kitchen is stocked[4] with food and there is a fridge[5] and microwave oven. There is a hot shower, and there are comfortable beds and lots of books, DVDs, and video games. Most guests, however, spend their time at one of the large windows watching angelfish, snappers, and barracudas swimming by.

---

3) lodge : n. a small house in the country where people stay when they want to take part in some types of outdoor sport. (행락지의) 여관, 소규모 별장.

4) stock : v. to keep a supply of a particular type of goods to sell. 쌓아두다.

5) fridge : n. a refrigerator, especially a household refrigerator. 냉장고.

The Best Hotel in the World

Many people consider Burj Al Arab in Dubai to be the best hotel in the world. It is designed to look like the sail of a ship, and at 321 meters tall, it is very impressive building. When it is lit up at night, it is an amazing sight.

The 5-star hotel does not have rooms. It has 202 suites[6], each made up of two floors. Each suite has its own reception desk, so you never need to visit reception. A team of butlers[7] provide a 24-hour-a-day service.

Each suite has a luxurious living area, a dining area with a bar, and an office area with a laptop and Internet access. You can operate the plasma screen TV, change the room temperature, or open and close the curtains just by touching a button. The floor-to-ceiling windows provide an incredible view of the coast.

6) suite : n. a set of rooms, especially in a hotel. 스위트룸(호텔의 침실 · 욕실 · 거실 등이 이어진 한 세트의 방).

7) butler : n. the main male servant in a large house. 집사.

Burj Al Arab has eight fantastic restaurants to choose from, and there is a cocktail bar and a cigar lounge. There is a health club, which has two swimming pools, a fitness center, a squash court, a sauna, a jacuzzi[8)] and massage rooms.

If you leave the hotel, you can lie on the beautiful private beach, play golf, go scuba diving, take a trip in a hot air balloon, or go on a desert safari. If you want to, you can order a Rolls Royce limousine with a chauffeur[9)] to drive you around.

– From *Essential Reading*, MacMillan

8) Jacuzzi : n. a large bath or pool with underwater jets that massage and invigorate the body. 거품 목욕탕.

9) chauffeur : n. a person whose job is to drive a car, especially for sb rich or important. 운전사.

Exercises

I. Read the following paragraph and answer the questions.

The Ice Hotel is in Jukkasjarvi, a village in Sweden 200 kilometers north of the Arctic Circle. Every winter, a team of architects, designers and snow builders build the hotel. This year there are 80 rooms. Everything is made of ice, which in this part of the world is crystal clear. The walls, the floors, the ceilings, and even the furniture are all made of ice. The beds are made of ice too, but guests sleep on warm reindeer skins.

1. Where is Jukkasjarvi located?
2. Who built this hotel?
3. How many rooms did they build?
4. What are made of ice in this hotel?
5. Where do the guests get to sleep?

II. Fill each blank with one of the words given below.

up	in	with	from	of

6. Guests must drive for miles through the jungle to find it (   ) the middle of a tea and coffee plantation.
7. Everything is made (   ) ice, which in this part of the world is crystal clear.
8. The hotel has a bar, where guest can drink vodka (   ) glasses made of ice.
9. the kitchen is stocked (   ) food and there is a fridge and microwave oven.
10. When it is lit (   ) at night, it is an amazing sight.

III. Match the word or expression with its definition.

11. ladder	a. a place to stay
12. fridge	b. a piece of equipment for climbing up and down a wall
13. chauffeur	c. a person who looks after guests in a hotel
14. lodge	d. a household refrigerator
15. butler	e. a person whose job is to drive a car

IV. Mark each sentence as either true(T) or false(F) according to the text.

16. Green Magic Tree House is easy to get to. (   )
17. It is warmer in the Ice Hotel than it is outside. (   )
18. If you want to stay at Jules Underwater Lodge, you need to swim under water. (   )
19. At Burj Al Arab it is easy to make the rooms in the suites warmer or cooler. (   )
20. You can do a lot of different sports inside and outside Burj Al Arab Hotel. (   )

V. Put these words from the box into the correct column.

chauffer / door / fish / window / fridge / bird / architect / wall / insect designer / bathroom / floor / microwave oven / ceiling / reindeer

parts of a building	kitchen appliances	living things	jobs